# EVIDENCE-BASED TEACHING for HIGHER EDUCATION

# EVIDENCE-BASED TEACHING for HIGHER EDUCATION

*Edited by*
Beth M. Schwartz
*and* Regan A. R. Gurung

AMERICAN PSYCHOLOGICAL ASSOCIATION
WASHINGTON, DC

Published by
American Psychological Association
750 First Street, NE
Washington, DC 20002
www.apa.org

To order
APA Order Department
P.O. Box 92984
Washington, DC 20090-2984
Tel: (800) 374-2721; Direct: (202) 336-5510
Fax: (202) 336-5502; TDD/TTY: (202) 336-6123
Online: www.apa.org/pubs/books
E-mail: order@apa.org

In the U.K., Europe, Africa, and the Middle East, copies may be ordered from
American Psychological Association
3 Henrietta Street
Covent Garden, London
WC2E 8LU England

Typeset in Goudy by Circle Graphics, Inc., Columbia, MD

Printer: Edwards Brothers, Inc., Ann Arbor, MI
Cover Designer: Berg Design, Albany, NY

**Library of Congress Cataloging-in-Publication Data**

Schwartz, Beth M.
  Evidence-based teaching for higher education / Beth M. Schwartz and Regan A. R. Gurung.
      p. cm
  Includes index.
  ISBN 978-1-4338-1172-2—ISBN 1-4338-1172-3 1. College teaching—Methodology.
2. College teaching—Psychological aspects. 3. Effective teaching. 4. Education, Higher—
United States. I. Gurung, Regan A. R. II. Title.
  LB2331.S375 2012
378.125—dc23
                                        2011053043

**British Library Cataloguing-in-Publication Data**
A CIP record is available from the British Library.

*Printed in the United States of America*
*First Edition*

DOI: 10.1037/13745-000

# CONTENTS

# CONTRIBUTORS

**Suzanne C. Baker, PhD,** James Madison University, Harrisonburg, VA
**William Buskist, PhD,** Auburn University, Auburn, AL
**Dana S. Dunn, PhD,** Moravian College, Bethlehem, PA
**Robert S. Feldman, PhD,** University of Massachusetts, Amherst
**Regan A. R. Gurung, PhD,** University of Wisconsin–Green Bay
**Jane S. Halonen, PhD,** University of West Florida, Pensacola
**R. Eric Landrum, PhD,** Boise State University, Boise, ID
**Angela M. Legg, PhD,** University of California, Riverside
**Ryan C. Martin, PhD,** University of Wisconsin–Green Bay
**Lee I. McCann, PhD,** University of Wisconsin–Oshkosh
**Maureen A. McCarthy, PhD,** Kennesaw State University, Kennesaw, GA
**Lawrence McGahey, PhD,** The College of St. Scholastica, Duluth, MN
**Chandra M. Mehrotra, PhD,** The College of St. Scholastica, Duluth, MN
**Christopher R. Poirier, PhD,** Stonehill College, Easton, MA
**Deirdre M. Radosevich, PhD,** University of Wisconsin–Green Bay
**Beth M. Schwartz, PhD,** Randolph College, Lynchburg, VA
**Randolph A. Smith, PhD,** Lamar University, Beaumont, TX

**Kristin M. Vespia, PhD,** University of Wisconsin–Green Bay
**Janie H. Wilson, PhD,** Georgia Southern University, Statesboro
**Shauna B. Wilson, PhD,** Florida State University, Tallahassee
**Georjeanna Wilson-Doenges, PhD,** University of Wisconsin–Green Bay

# FOREWORD

WILLIAM BUSKIST

I started my academic career in the days when teachers would either write their notes out longhand or peck them out on a typewriter. At that time, a few faculty had computers in their offices, but powerful teaching tools like PowerPoint, Blackboard, and the Internet were still decades away from appearing on the academic scene. Students came to class with only notebooks and pencils and not wireless laptops, cell phones, and MP3 players. Armed with only the most modest of learning technologies, students attending class had few alternatives to listening to the lecturer and jotting down occasional notes.

In fact, at the time, faculty seemingly had few alternatives to lecturing. Like most new teachers "back in the day," I taught by lecturing because that's all I knew to do. No one took me aside and talked to me about how to teach, or why teaching was an important, let alone a noble, endeavor. So, because all my teachers had taught via the lecture, I did too. Nonetheless, a few exceedingly brave, creative, and innovative teachers like Fred Keller[1] dared experiment with new teaching methods that focused more on getting

---

[1]Keller, F. S. (1968). "Good-bye teacher . . ." *Journal of Applied Behavior Analysis*, *1*, 79–80. doi:10.1901/jaba.1968.1.79

students engaged in the learning process than on delivering polished lectures. Although Keller and others like him didn't know it at the time, they were introducing the rest of us to what we today call *active learning*.

How fortunate we are now to live and work during an era in which we not only enjoy the unparalleled benefits of applying modern technology to help us teach and students learn, but in which we also have a growing understanding of the relationship between effective teaching and student learning. Indeed, the last 2 decades have witnessed tremendous advances in the scholarship of teaching and learning (SoTL). As a result of this sustained and rigorous empirical study of teaching methodology, course design, student study practices, and the assessment of student learning outcomes, we possess a deep, although still incomplete, knowledge of teaching habits and practices that can, and do, enhance student learning. One of the most important findings to emerge from this literature is that the best learning—the deepest, most meaningful, and longest lasting form of learning—accrues to the learner as a result of being somehow *actively* involved in the learning process. As each chapter in this book demonstrates, such active involvement is a key to any and all aspects of effective teaching and learning.

Interestingly, though, a lot of what we know empirically about teaching and learning has yet to make it into the hands of many, perhaps even most, college and university teachers. Thus, some teachers may teach well, but with little understanding of why their methods are effective or how to make them more effective. Even worse, some teachers are unaware that evidence-based approaches to teaching even exist. A large part of this problem is due, I think, to the relative dearth of books and other publications that summarize, integrate, or otherwise pull together the empirical literature in ways that are immediately adaptable to everyday teaching. Although it is true that many "how to" teaching books for college and university teaching are readily available, these books tend to focus primarily on telling the reader how to implement particular teaching methods without accounting for, or otherwise explaining, their effectiveness for enhancing student learning. Such an approach may be helpful in the short run in terms of creating teaching technicians—teachers who can follow instructions in how to implement a particular teaching strategy in their classrooms. Unfortunately, it does little in the short or the long run to truly advance the science of teaching—to encourage faculty to become teaching scholars—teachers who adopt a teaching methodology on the basis of empirical evidence and then systematically investigate how that methodology impacts student learning.

Therein rests the importance of this book. The editors have assembled an excellent cast of authors—a most talented group of teacher–scholars who are intimately conversant with the SoTL literature. On the basis of a combination of empirical evidence, their teaching expertise, and their classroom experience, these authors blend SoTL research and theory with practice, creating a compelling volume that provides cutting-edge strategies for improving readers' teaching skills and enhancing their students' learning. As an added bonus, the editors and authors implicitly invite readers to discover, and take advantage of, the bountiful opportunities for engaging in SoTL research as a part of the adventure that is teaching.

I thoroughly enjoyed and benefitted enormously from reading this book. To be sure, although I started teaching in the dark ages before the microchip, this book has taught me that I still have much to learn about making sound, evidence-based pedagogical choices. It also helped remind me of why teaching is important—because it has the potential to make a difference in the lives and well-being of our students.

# ACKNOWLEDGMENTS

A number of individuals made valuable contributions during the development, writing, and editing of this book. We owe special thanks to Linda Malnasi McCarter, senior acquisitions editor at the American Psychological Association (APA), for her enthusiasm and continued support of this project from our initial discussions of the idea to the final editing stages. We also thank Beth Hatch at APA Books for her valuable guidance through the review and editing process. We received very helpful feedback from reviewers, including Barney Beins and Stephen Chew, whose comments facilitated changes that allowed us to meet our original goal for the book. A number of our students were also involved in the development and editing process, including Carl Coffey, Alexis Mandarakas, and Jerry Wells from Randolph College. Our sincere gratitude goes out to our families, whose support is always crucial when in the midst of deadlines and rewrites, as we attempt to continue to meet our responsibilities to all of those we care deeply about at home. We are especially grateful for the support and encouragement of our friends in the Society for the Teaching of Psychology, whose mission to foster the scholarship of teaching and learning fueled our passion to do the same. Last, but not least, we thank all of the contributors who took the time to write and rewrite their chapters so that readers can benefit from a book that speaks the same language and in turn provides readers with valuable information on each pedagogical issue in question. We hope this evidence-based resource will provide faculty members with the knowledge needed to continue to improve the learning environment for the many students who enter their classrooms.

# EVIDENCE-BASED TEACHING for HIGHER EDUCATION

# INTRODUCTION

BETH M. SCHWARTZ AND REGAN A. R. GURUNG

When designing a course and even preparing for a class meeting, university teachers must always decide how to engage students and what strategies will best aid learning. How do these teachers decide whether to lecture or use small group discussions, or whether to provide students with notes for the day? How do they incorporate experiential learning into the courses? How do they choose textbooks for their courses, organize the first day of class, and incorporate technology into the classroom? Although university teachers have advanced degrees in their content area, few have much training in teaching, and even fewer have the time to find empirical research to guide their pedagogical choices. As a result, most teachers choose techniques and tools on the basis of how well these techniques and tools seemed to work the last time they were used or how the instructor was taught the material when he or she was a student.

A growing body of psychological research has provided empirical evidence on how teachers teach and students learn. This research, known to many as the *scholarship of teaching and learning* (SoTL), is primarily conducted by college and university professors. Many SoTL studies are conducted by psychology professors using university psychology class samples. However, teachers from all disciplines conduct SoTL, and the findings are relevant to university teachers in all disciplines.

Findings from the SoTL literature can be invaluable when developing a new course, deciding how to teach particular course content, or invigorating a previously taught course. Yet, although many guides are available on how to conduct SoTL (e.g., Gurung & Schwartz, 2009; McKinney, 2007), few resources are available that summarize the empirical findings of SoTL and can guide an instructor in choosing teaching techniques and tools that are based on data-driven evidence. This edited volume fills the gap by synthesizing SoTL findings to help teachers choose teaching techniques and tools. It will also help faculty determine how to approach SoTL research on particular pedagogical issues on the basis of what is already known from the literature by clearly identifying the gaps in the SoTL literature.

To provide the most up-to-date empirical evidence, we have asked the authors of each chapter—who are all experts in the SoTL field and strong teachers—to summarize the findings for a particular pedagogical issue, to provide specific recommendations regarding the use of a particular technique or tool, and to identify what remains unknown in the SoTL field. Each chapter will allow faculty to go beyond what is thought to be the most effective techniques and tools. Rather than reliance on memory for what worked the last time we taught the material, or what others have advised when it comes to covering certain content, we can now base pedagogical decisions on the findings from SoTL.

This book will be an important resource for all university teachers, as well as for professionals who work in university faculty development centers. For new teachers, this book will provide an important starting point to facilitate thinking beyond content, which is often the orientation one has after just completing a graduate degree. It will go beyond the how-tos of teaching a course, addressing more detailed issues, such as when to choose a particular technique over another and how to base that decision on findings from the SoTL literature. For faculty who have taught before and are facing reappointment, tenure, or promotion, this book will help explain to review committees why pedagogical choices are made in the classroom and how those choices are based on empirical evidence. Finally, this book can be a valuable resource for university faculty development centers, which often work with faculty to maximize teaching effectiveness. Directors of these centers can incorporate findings from this book into teaching workshops, as well as into consultations with individual faculty members.

This book is organized into eight chapters. Chapter 1 provides a brief history of SoTL; specifies how SoTL benefits students, faculty, departments, and institutions; and addresses the common question concerning whether SoTL differs from traditional research. Chapter 2 addresses important questions related to instructors' classroom rapport with students, identifying what influences the first impressions made and what challenges exist to building rapport between students and instructors. In Chapter 3, readers learn the best practices concerning the use of technology in the classroom, including audience response systems, podcasting, blogs, wikis, and more. Chapter 4 reviews the factors one needs to take into account when designing and teaching an online course, including, for example, the many instructional choices particular to this method of teaching, how to best assess student learning, and the characteristics of successful online students. Chapter 5 covers experiential learning, addressing different approaches such as service learning, internships, teaching assistantships, and classroom research. In addition to a discussion of the evidence-based best practices for each approach, this chapter also includes the important question of evaluation of student learning for each of these methods. Chapter 6 turns to the important question of students' study strategies. Readers will learn how to improve class materials and preparation and what advice to give students when it comes to choosing the most effective study strategies. Chapter 7 provides advice on textbook selection, examines the many variables that differentiate one textbook from another, and considers the alternative of using readings instead of textbooks. Finally, Chapter 8 addresses the issue of documenting teaching effectiveness. Readers will learn about the challenges and strategies associated with self-assessment, the role of student feedback, and how to create documentation beyond student evaluations that will be most useful for tenure and promotion.

The goal of this book is twofold: (a) to identify practical, evidence-supported strategies that teachers can use to maximize teaching effectiveness and student learning and (b) to stimulate future SoTL research. Toward this end, each chapter ends with a succinct list of teaching recommendations that are based on the empirical evidence presented in the chapter, followed by a succinct list of questions that future SoTL research should investigate.

## REFERENCES

Gurung, R. A. R., & Schwartz, B. M. (2009). *Optimizing teaching and learning: Pedagogical research in practice*. Malden, MA: Blackwell.

McKinney, K. (2007). *Enhancing learning through the scholarship of teaching and learning: The challenges and joys of juggling*. Bolton, MA: Anker.

# 1

# BENEFITS OF USING SoTL IN PICKING AND CHOOSING PEDAGOGY

RANDOLPH A. SMITH

The scholarship of teaching and learning (SoTL) has a short history but a long past. More specifically, the formal recognition of SoTL is not very old, but the activities that make up SoTL have been going on for quite some time. Although some readers of this volume may be familiar with SoTL, I provide a brief history in the following section.

## EARLY HISTORY OF SoTL

Ernest Boyer (1990) is typically credited with beginning the current SoTL movement with his book *Scholarship Reconsidered*. However, I would argue that Boyer helped brand a movement that was already ongoing and evolving (see Gurung & Schwartz, 2009, 2010). My interpretation of Boyer's goal is that he wished to raise the prominence of teaching in academia. He noted, "Almost all colleges pay lip service to the trilogy of teaching, research, and service, but when it comes to making judgments about professional performance, the three are rarely assigned equal merit" (p. 15). Boyer sensed a crisis in the academy regarding the lack of attention paid to teaching.

In an attempt to remedy the problem of teaching playing second fiddle to research, Boyer (1990) argued that the meaning of *scholarship* should be broadened to encompass more than research. Boyer proposed four types of scholarship. The *scholarship of discovery* encompasses what academics currently refer to as research. The other scholarships that Boyer proposed, however, were new to the academy. The *scholarship of integration* refers to multidisciplinary work, merging traditional research into larger intellectual patterns or focusing on the meaning of research findings. The *scholarship of application*, as its name implies, refers to applying research findings to the real world in an attempt to solve problems. Finally, Boyer proposed adding the *scholarship of teaching* to academic life. In this formulation, Boyer meant much more than the simple transmitting of facts to learners. Good teachers "stimulate active, not passive, learning and encourage students to be critical, creative thinkers, with the capacity to go on learning after their college days are over" (p. 24).

## SCHOLARLY TEACHING AND THE SCHOLARSHIP OF TEACHING

Boyer's (1990) work on the scholarship of teaching has been highly influential within academia. The term gained traction in psychology with the work by a task force of the Society for the Teaching of Psychology's publication defining scholarship in psychology (Halpern et al., 1998). However, it has also undergone some transition over the years. One major development is the addition of a related term: Glassick, Huber, and Maeroff (1997) wrote a follow-up to Boyer's (1990) book in which they used the term *scholarly teaching* (p. 10), apparently equating that term with the scholarship of teaching. Rather than finding these terms synonymous, however, I favor Richlin's (2001) conceptualization of scholarly teaching contrasted with the scholarship of teaching. As teachers, we often "experiment" with the classes we teach. We typically tweak various assignments, lectures, and calendar arrangements in an attempt to make the class better than the last time. Making such changes is a common approach for teachers who are concerned about their teaching. Richlin described a scholarly teacher as one who takes this revision process a step further and is more intentional about making changes, tackling the process in a logical, systematic process. As Figure 1.1 shows, engaging in scholarly teaching is much like beginning a typical research project. Scholarly teachers consult the available literature before making any change to a course. They systematically gather and analyze data to discover whether the change did indeed make a difference. This systematic approach contrasts sharply with the intuitive type of process first described.

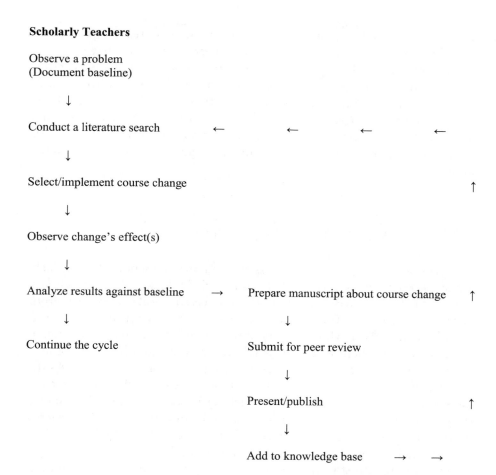

**Scholarly Teachers**

Observe a problem
(Document baseline)

↓

Conduct a literature search      ←      ←      ←      ←

↓

Select/implement course change                             ↑

↓

Observe change's effect(s)

↓

Analyze results against baseline   →    Prepare manuscript about course change   ↑

↓                                ↓

Continue the cycle                  Submit for peer review

↓

Present/publish                           ↑

↓

Add to knowledge base      →      →

**Scholarship of Teaching/Learning**

*Figure 1.1.* Richlin's conceptualization of scholarly teaching leading to the scholarship of teaching and learning. From *Scholarship Revisited: Perspectives on the Scholarship of Teaching* (p. 59), by C. Kreber (Ed.), 2001, San Francisco, CA: Jossey-Bass. Copyright 2001 by John Wiley & Sons. Adapted with permission.

As praiseworthy as scholarly teaching is, I do not believe it represents what Boyer (1990) had in mind when he wrote about the scholarship of teaching. Richlin (2001) captured the distinction between scholarly teaching and the scholarship of teaching well (see Figure 1.1). Scholarly teachers who wish to translate their work into scholarship of teaching must follow the same process that other researchers do: They prepare a manuscript and submit their work for critical review and possible publication. If their work is published, it becomes part of the available scholarship regarding teaching, which transforms the scholarly teacher into a scholar of teaching and learning. Thus, teachers can consult the SoTL work of others as they engage in either scholarly teaching or scholarship of teaching. This outcome captures perfectly the goal of this volume; the hope is to provide readers with teaching-related best practices to use when facing various issues in teaching, choosing particular pedagogical tools, deciding how to assess a particular teaching method, deciding how to use and implement relevant research findings in the classroom, and identifying areas in which additional SoTL research is most needed.

## SCHOLARSHIP OF TEACHING MORPHS INTO SCHOLARSHIP OF TEACHING AND LEARNING

The scholarship of teaching has evolved into the scholarship of teaching *and learning,* more commonly known as SoTL (also referred to as *classroom research* by Cross & Steadman, 1996, and *pedagogical research* by Gurung & Schwartz, 2009, 2010). This change may have been sparked by Hutchings and Shulman (1999), who wrote about the confusion surrounding the differences among excellent teaching, scholarly teaching, and the scholarship of teaching. The reason for adding "and learning" is abundantly clear: As the practice of assessment has gained strength over the past 2 decades, the focus has shifted from the faculty member teaching a course to the students taking the course (Bain, 2004). As far as assessment is concerned, what the teacher does is of no consequence if students do not learn. A review of teaching-related articles shows the focus progressing from solely on the teacher or the activity (often with student satisfaction or enjoyment as an outcome measure) to a dual focus on the teacher/activity and student learning. Thus, to get published today, authors must typically demonstrate that students learned important information about the subject matter in addition to viewing the project in a positive light.

Looking back, SoTL has had a short history—the term has evolved from Boyer's (1990) coining of the term *scholarship of teaching.* In only 20 years, the term has gone through both evolution and greater specification (for more views on this topic, see Dunn, 2008; Irons & Buskist, 2008; Pan, 2009; Smith, 2008). However, the impact of SoTL on academia in that short time has been impressive. For example, as early as 1994, the Carnegie Foundation National Survey on the Reexamination of Faculty Roles and Rewards reported that 78% of provosts agreed that the definition of *scholarship* was being broadened to include the full range of activities in which faculty were engaged at their institution. The same survey showed that 62% of institutions reported that *Scholarship Reconsidered* (Boyer, 1990) had played a role in discussing faculty roles and rewards (Glassick et al., 1997)—even though the survey took place only less than 4 years after the book's publication.

The impact of this philosophical shift started by Boyer (1990) is evident in the field of psychology. Gurung, Ansburg, Alexander, Lawrence, and Johnson (2008) conducted a national survey of psychology faculty, with 142 responses divided relatively evenly by rank and type of institution. Respondents indicated that their departments had faculty members involved in SoTL (60.9% *agreed* or *strongly agreed*), their department norms encouraged SoTL work (55.0%), their department viewed SoTL work favorably when evaluating job candidates (67.4%), and their department chair encouraged involvement in SoTL (60.0%). Institution-wide support for SoTL, as reported by individual faculty, was somewhat lower but still present. When it came to important decisions, respondents indicated that criteria for promotion reflected principles of SoTL (54.3% departmental, 47.9% institutional) and that faculty members in their departments had received tenure based at least in part on SoTL (61.1% departmental, 65.4% institutional). Gurung et al. found that faculty respondents perceived two major obstacles to involving more faculty in SoTL: confusion among faculty about what constitutes SoTL (73.1% agreed or strongly agreed) and many faculty members' perception that SoTL is an addition to their workload (80.0%). Although it is clear that SoTL work is not universally valued and rewarded (Glassick et al., 1997; Gurung et al., 2008; Huber & Hutchings, 2005), there is a significant portion of psychology departments and institutions that do find value in such work.

## BENEFITS OF USING SoTL RESEARCH

In this section, I examine the benefits to various audiences that accrue through the use of SoTL research. To clarify, I am referring to situations in which faculty members use the results of SoTL research rather than engaging in SoTL themselves. Remember that Richlin (2001) noted that scholarly teachers consult the literature before choosing and applying an intervention in their classes (see Figure 1.1). Gurung and Schwartz (2010) referred to this process as catalyzing SoTL use or providing/modeling ways that faculty can use SoTL. Thus, by referring to SoTL research, I refer to the process of faculty reading and evaluating the research literature on teaching, either in their discipline or around the type of teaching they wish to pursue. Note that mere reading of literature is not enough—the scholarly teacher must use critical thinking to evaluate that literature to determine its soundness and validity (see Gurung, 2012, for ideas about the ethical use of evidence-based pedagogy). This process is no different than faculty members reading any research literature to determine whether it is worthy of inclusion in their research agenda.

There is some debate about what qualifies as SoTL research. Some people or disciplines may endorse any type of teaching-related writing as SoTL. Although there is potential value in any type of pedagogical research, the stakes have risen over the years in terms of the type of evidence readers, reviewers, and editors want to see. Although it may still be possible to publish anecdotal accounts of "this is what I did in my class, and it worked" or teaching activities that students like and believed helped them learn, I would discount those types of reports as fitting into the SoTL framework. At the same time, I do not believe it is "fair" to expect SoTL research to use the most stringent experimental designs such as random assignment to groups or controlling all extraneous variables. It is a fact of life that pedagogical research is likely to be somewhat "messy," without being able to institute all the experimental design procedures that laboratory research demands. It is not too much to expect, however, that good SoTL research is able to pinpoint increases in learning on the part of students as likely being a function of the pedagogical variable that the researcher has studied. This impact on learning, to me, is what defines SoTL research.

## Benefits to the Students

Given that SoTL aims to improve the learning of students, it is predictable that students who take courses from SoTL-oriented faculty should benefit in some way. Students should have a reasonable expectation of effective, enthusiastic faculty using empirically tested teaching approaches.

### Assurance of Learning

The primary benefit that students derive from courses taught by faculty who are using SoTL research in their teaching is assurance of learning. Teaching that is based on SoTL research has undergone scrutiny by the faculty member involved, as well as by peers during the review process. The teaching activities, exercises, and approaches used by the faculty member have demonstrated effectiveness in a classroom setting. When faculty are using state-of-the-art instructional methods and students actually give effort, learning should occur. For example, Berry and Chew (2008) conducted SoTL research by class-testing two learning strategies derived from laboratory research and demonstrated Daniel and Poole's (2009) point that results from the lab can also have pedagogical implications. One strategy involved having students submit questions for extra credit about material covered between the second and third exams. Students who submitted questions had lower scores on the first exam than students who did not submit questions. However, scores on the third exam did not differ between the students who did and did not submit questions, thus demonstrating that asking questions helped low-performing students raise their scores. The second strategy involved constructing concept maps about course material, again between the second and third exams. Although there was no difference in scores on the first two exams for students who did or did not submit concept maps, students who submitted concept maps outscored their counterparts on the third exam. Thus, students who learned about asking questions or constructing concept maps about the material they covered can reasonably expect to learn and retain more of the material.

Another way that faculty can provide assurance of learning is by instituting class policies supported by pedagogical research. For example, if a professor could cite well-done research showing that students who text in class performed more poorly than students who do not text, the professor would have a valid reason for prohibiting texting during class. It also stands to reason that students would react more positively to such a prohibition if there is research supporting it than if the students perceive the prohibition as an arbitrary rule imposed by an out-of-touch faculty member. For example, Fried (2008) conducted a classroom study of laptop use and found a negative relation with several measures of student learning. Thus, instructors could legitimately ban laptop use in their classes and cite data for why they have such a rule. Likewise, if a statistics instructor requires students to complete homework assignments, they are less likely to view the problems as busy work if the instructor can cite research showing that students learn statistics better by completing homework problems.

*Effective, Enthusiastic Faculty*

For years, administrators have justified requiring faculty engagement in scholarship with the belief that conducting research makes for better and more enthusiastic faculty. If that justification is true, how much more true is it that faculty will be effective in and enthusiastic about using techniques in class that they have studied and tested themselves? Buskist, Sikorski, Buckley, and Saville (2002) demonstrated that enthusiasm is one of the top 10 characteristics of master teachers as rated by both students and faculty. Interestingly, Tomcho and Foels (2008), after a large-scale meta-analysis of teaching activities published in *Teaching of Psychology* from 1974 to 2006, wrote that variables such as rapport, immediacy, and working alliance, which likely feed into teacher enthusiasm, may be important for the effectiveness of those activities. Also on Buskist et al.'s list of characteristics of master teachers, "knowledgeable about topic" ranked second by students and first by faculty. Clearly, faculty members using approaches in the classroom that they have pioneered or studied experimentally will be quite knowledgeable about the topic.

## Benefits to the Faculty Member

Just as students derive benefits from faculty who use SoTL-based teaching practices, the teachers themselves should expect to benefit also. Faculty can assure themselves that they are using classroom best practices and that they should have students who will learn more.

### Best Practices

Faculty who rely on SoTL research to find and implement classroom techniques and activities can assure themselves that they are engaging in best practices in the classroom. Just as therapists and MDs would not use treatments that had not been validated, conscientious teachers should endeavor to use teaching approaches on which they know they can rely. As practitioners in medicine, clinical psychology, health psychology, and the like move toward evidence-based treatment approaches (e.g., Cochrane, 1972; Melnyk & Fineout-Overholt, 2005), shouldn't faculty take the same approach? To help faculty choose such approaches, the Society for the Teaching of Psychology began a series of Best Practices conferences in 2002, spotlighting such topics as educational assessment, introductory psychology, research methods and statistics, culture and diversity, critical thinking, beginning (e.g., introductory, orientation to the major) and ending (e.g., capstone, research intensive, seminar) courses, and teaching with technology. In order to allow faculty everywhere to benefit from these conferences, an edited book has grown out of each conference (Dunn, Beins, McCarthy, & Hill, 2010; Dunn & Chew, 2006; Dunn, Halonen, & Smith, 2008; Dunn, Mehrotra, & Halonen, 2004; Dunn, Smith, & Beins, 2007; Dunn, Wilson, Freeman, & Stowell, 2011; Dunn, Wilson, Gurung, & Naufel, in press; Gurung & Prieto, 2009). The organizers of each conference evaluated the conference proceedings and asked faculty with the topics that typified the best practices notion to author chapters for the books.

### Student Learning

Not only will faculty know that they are using best practices, but they will also benefit by having students who will likely learn more. Students who learn more are likely to be more successful in a particular course, which likely leads to greater satisfaction and happiness with both the instructor and the course. As any faculty member can attest, having students who are more successful, satisfied, and happy in a class is a desirable combination. Gurung and Vespia (2007), for example, measured students' perceptions of 10 variables concerning instructor and classes. The highest correlation (.82) they found among all the variables was between students' perceived learning and enjoyment of a class. Tomcho and Foels (2008) conducted a meta-analysis of almost 200 published studies evaluating teaching activities and methods. They found an average of a medium effect size for the activities.

### Benefit to the Department and Institution

It is hard to imagine in this day and age that there are any departments or colleges that have not been affected by the assessment movement. Regional accrediting agencies have been a major player in pushing the assessment agenda, as they have placed a premium on student learning as a criterion for accreditation. In times of tight budgets, state legislatures, governing boards, and parents have also demanded greater accountability regarding student learning. By using class-tested, valid teaching methods, faculty and departments will be more easily able to demonstrate student achievement for assessment reports. In my experience, psychology faculty tend to be more open to assessment requirements than some other disciplines, thus making many psychology departments good role models for meaningful assessment plans. Therefore, psychology faculty and departments are often institutional leaders in assessment planning and implementation. This type of leadership is appreciated and (sometimes) rewarded by administrators such as deans and provosts. The next section focuses on some of the potential rewards that can come from such work.

### Summary

After reading about the benefits of using SoTL research, I hope that it is clear what advice I would give to faculty members. If you are not yet engaging in scholarly teaching, I heartily recommend that you begin. Today, there is certainly an abundance of teaching-related research available. It is not difficult to find recommendations regarding best practices in many different areas of teaching. Rather than relying on gut feelings or instinct, you should plunge into the teaching literature to see what is available. Revise your teaching practices so that they are in line with research-based recommendations so that you can engage in scholarly teaching. You, your students, and your department and institution will all benefit from such a change.

## BENEFITS OF ENGAGING IN SoTL WORK

Most of the benefits of actually doing SoTL research accrue directly to the faculty members doing that research. Although I list several possible benefits in the following paragraphs, I suspect that there are also idiosyncratic benefits of engaging in SoTL. Just as faculty engage in laboratory research for a variety of reasons and find a variety of reinforcements in that work, they also engage in SoTL work in the same manner.

## Tenure and Promotion

Although the data I cited earlier indicated that not all departments or institutions value SoTL work for tenure and promotion, it appears that over half of these academic units do count SoTL work toward these faculty rewards (Glassick et al., 1997). Thus, faculty who conduct research that will benefit them and their students in the classroom also stand to make progress toward tenure and promotion at their institutions. Depending on the given institution, SoTL-related publications and even conference presentations may carry weight toward such professional advancement. Given that tenure and promotion are typically tied to salary and raises, there is possibly even more of a payoff for engaging in SoTL research.

## Professional Recognition and Standing

Faculty members who publish SoTL work over time may become known as assessment or SoTL experts within their disciplines. Developing such a reputation can lead to many professional opportunities, which can enhance one's professional standing. For example, I know faculty who have developed such reputations who have been asked to serve as keynote speakers at assessment-related (or other) conferences, write chapters for books (such as this one), serve as outside reviewers for departments, consult with departments or universities on their assessment plans, serve as reviewers on regional accreditation teams, and so on. Such activities not only enhance the faculty member's professional reputation but also are typically viewed favorably by one's home institution, thus feeding into the tenure, promotion, and merit-pay decisions.

In addition, becoming well-known as an expert on SoTL can lead to opportunities to serve in leadership positions in organizations that focus on SoTL, assessment, and other similar activities. For example, faculty with such expertise may be asked to serve on editorial boards of publications that focus on such work (e.g., *International Journal for the Scholarship of Teaching and Learning*, *Journal on Excellence in College Teaching*, or one of the many disciplinary journals that focus on or include SoTL work). They might be elected to serve as officers in organizations that include SoTL, assessment, or student learning in their areas of focus or serve on conference-organizing committees for meetings such as the STP Best Practices conferences. Again, it is likely that these types of activities will be viewed favorably by the faculty's home institution.

## Administrative Responsibilities

Faculty who produce SoTL-based scholarship may have chances to take on administrative positions at departmental or college levels. Speaking from the perspective of a department chair, it is essential rather than a luxury to have a faculty member who is willing to serve as the departmental assessment coordinator. Chairs have a multitude of duties to perform; if departmental assessment is included on that long list, then it is unlikely to get the full attention that it merits. Faculty who are assessment savvy and assessment oriented have a chance to take on a departmental assignment of coordinating assessment that involves some degree of administrative work. There might even be a chance to become the assessment coordinator for the entire college or university. Some faculty are curious about becoming involved in administrative work, so this type of position would allow them to "get their feet wet" without fully committing to administration by becoming a chair. At the very least, there are likely positions to be filled on an assessment committee at departmental, college, or university levels.

## Benefit to the Larger Academic Community

Although most of the benefits of conducting SoTL research accrue to the individual faculty members involved, there is one major benefit that applies to academia in general. As Bernstein (2002) noted, "Talented people find ingenious solutions to problems in learning every academic term, and traditionally most of that work is lost" (p. 228). This statement is a powerful argument that although scholarly teaching is a good and necessary step for teachers to take, it is simply not enough. Engaging in SoTL work keeps the knowledge about teaching from being lost. It is imperative to build a body of knowledge concerning best practices in teaching just as scholars build a body of knowledge concerning other research areas. Researchers do not have to reinvent the wheel time after time; teachers should not have to do so either. If I am teaching a new course for the first time, or if I have a topic that I find particularly difficult to get across to my students, I should be able to conduct a literature search and find answers to my questions regarding how to teach in these situations. Many journals are devoted to or include SoTL work (see Gurung & Schwartz, 2009); college teaching centers may include such a listing on their website. Teachers can also attend SoTL-related conferences as a means of gathering information that could be relevant to their use of SoTL in the classroom (Gurung & Schwartz, 2009, p. 83). Several websites list conferences dedicated to SoTL (e.g., http://academics.georgiasouthern.edu/ijsotl/conference/2011/; http://www.issotl.org/; http://teachpsych.org/conferences/index.php).

EXHIBIT 1.1
Evidence-Based Recommendations

- When conducting SoTL, take a much more intentional approach than the typical "experiments" that all teachers take with their classes on a regular basis in an attempt to improve them.
- Thoroughly review the literature before beginning an SoTL project.
- Strive to develop comparable groups for comparison purposes.
- Although student enjoyment and satisfaction are important variables, focus on the actual learning of students.
- To move your research from scholarly teaching to SoTL, submit the research for peer review and present/publish the findings.

## Summary

After they review the benefits of engaging in SoTL work, my advice to faculty members is fairly predictable. After making the change to scholarly teaching, I advise you to consider beginning a line of research that is based on SoTL. This step will help you become a more effective teacher because you will find out whether your students benefit and learn more from strategies that you (or other teachers) have developed. Thus, rather than merely reading about other faculty members' research, you can create your own research. Engaging in such work can result in many benefits for you. Review the SoTL best practices summarized in Exhibit 1.1 as you get started.

## DOES SoTL RESEARCH DIFFER FROM TRADITIONAL RESEARCH?

The short answer to this question is yes . . . and no. By necessity, SoTL research, indeed any pedagogical research, must differ from traditional lab research. As I wrote earlier in the chapter, it is a fact of life that pedagogical research is likely to be somewhat messy, without being able to institute all the experimental design procedures that carefully controlled laboratory research demands. Is this difficulty a slap at or a death blow for SoTL research? If a researcher answered yes to that question, then that researcher would be damning much of the real-world applied research that goes on. As I ask my students when teaching about descriptive and correlational research approaches, does our lack of the ability to establish cause-and-effect explanations about variables such as sex and personality mean that we should give up and not study those topics? Of course not—and it should be the same with studying the effects of teaching and learning.

There are ways in which SoTL research does not differ from traditional research. As Richlin (2001) noted, a scholarly teacher goes through the same steps in designing classroom interventions that researchers in other areas use: finding a problem or question, establishing a baseline, consulting the research literature, choosing and applying an intervention, measuring and documenting observations, analyzing the results, and comparing them to the baseline. For SoTL, researchers submit their results to peer review—when published, their data and conclusions become part of the knowledge base about teaching and learning. Also, given some ingenuity, it may be possible to arrive at causal explanations despite the messiness of classroom research. Although it is virtually impossible to randomly assign students to sections (groups), equivalence between two sections of students can be established through measurement of potential extraneous variables such as "intelligence" (SAT or ACT scores) and time of day (two sections of the same course taught at the same or similar times). Another strategy for establishing equivalence between students would be to match class sections on relevant variables. Although random assignment still helps to establish equivalence of groups on unknown variables, establishing group equivalence on important potential extraneous variables goes a long way toward creating equal groups. In similar fashion, although establishing perfect control groups may not be possible, using comparison groups of students from a previous semester or a colleague's section of the same or a similar course may allow you to make comparisons between groups that allow you to begin to draw tentative conclusions about a teaching intervention. Thus, the research approach to SoTL uses the same approaches as more traditional research areas to the greatest extent possible.

## FUTURE DIRECTIONS FOR SoTL/PEDAGOGICAL RESEARCH

One advantage for faculty who wish to get involved in conducting SoTL or pedagogical research is that this area is a somewhat recent development, as the history covered in this chapter has shown. Hence, there are numerous lines of research to which faculty can contribute. The trend of assessing student learning as a function of various pedagogies is so recent that it provides almost limitless opportunities for research.

More specifically, there are several topic areas that are in great need of empirical research. Although it seems logical that SoTL research would be positively linked to assessment outcomes, I am aware of no research demonstrating such a link. Another fruitful area for research is applying research findings from the laboratory to the real world of classrooms to determine whether the principles found in the lab are effective for student learning. Finally, there seems to be a dearth of theoretical models

EXHIBIT 1.2
Questions for Future Research

- Are SoTL and assessment outcomes linked?
- Are the laboratory results regarding effects on learning and cognition generalizable to real-life situations such as classrooms?
- What theories can account for SoTL findings?

dealing with student learning that would enable faculty to make meaningful predictions about the effects of their pedagogical strategies in the classroom. Development of such theoretical models would advance the science of SoTL and help give it more widespread credibility throughout the academy. Exhibit 1.2 provides a summary of these suggested directions for SoTL research.

## CONCLUSION

Although the enterprise of SoTL is relatively young, it has a somewhat long and interesting history. Many benefits accrue from using and engaging in SoTL work. To the truly dedicated teacher, the bottom line could well be, "Can I help my students learn more?" Another important question is, "Do I have an ethical responsibility to help identify or develop best practices for teaching?" By engaging in SoTL-based research and using those results in the classroom, the dedicated teacher can be assured that the answer to those questions is a resounding yes!

## REFERENCES

Bain, K. (2004). *What the best college teachers do*. Cambridge, MA: Harvard University Press.

Bernstein, D. J. (2002). Representing the intellectual work in teaching through peer-reviewed course portfolios. In S. F. Davis & W. Buskist (Eds.), *The teaching of psychology: Essays in honor of Wilbert J. McKeachie and Charles L. Brewer* (pp. 215–229). Mahwah, NJ: Erlbaum.

Berry, J. W., & Chew, S. L. (2008). Improving learning through interventions of student-generated questions and concept maps. *Teaching of Psychology, 35*, 305–312. doi:10.1080/00986280802373841

Boyer, E. L. (1990). *Scholarship reconsidered: Priorities of the professoriate*. Princeton, NJ: The Carnegie Foundation for the Advancement of Teaching.

Buskist, W., Sikorski, J., Buckley, T., & Saville, B. K. (2002). Elements of master teaching. In S. F. Davis & W. Buskist (Eds.), *The teaching of psychology: Essays in honor of Wilbert J. McKeachie and Charles L. Brewer* (pp. 27–39). Mahwah, NJ: Erlbaum.

Cochrane, A. L. (1972). *Effectiveness and efficiency: Random reflections on health services.* London, England: Nuffield Provincial Hospitals Trust.

Cross, K. P., & Steadman, M. H. (1996). *Classroom research: Implementing the scholarship of teaching.* San Francisco, CA: Jossey-Bass.

Daniel, D. B., & Poole, D. A. (2009). Learning for life: An ecological approach to pedagogical research. *Perspectives on Psychological Science, 4,* 91–96. doi:10.1111/j.1745-6924.2009.01095.x

Dunn, D. S. (2008). Another view: In defense of vigor over rigor in classroom demonstrations. *Teaching of Psychology, 35,* 349–352. doi:10.1080/00986280802374039

Dunn, D. S., Beins, B. C., McCarthy, M. A., & Hill, G. W., IV. (2010). *Best practices for beginnings and endings in the psychology major.* New York, NY: Oxford University Press.

Dunn, D. S., & Chew, S. L. (2006). *Best practices for teaching introduction to psychology.* Mahwah, NJ: Erlbaum.

Dunn, D. S., Halonen, J. S., & Smith, R. A. (Eds.). (2008). *Teaching critical thinking in psychology: A handbook of best practices.* Malden, MA: Wiley-Blackwell. doi:10.1002/9781444305173

Dunn, D. S., Mehrotra, C., & Halonen, J. S. (Eds.). (2004). *Measuring up: Educational assessment challenges and practices for psychology.* Washington, DC: American Psychological Association. doi:10.1037/10807-000

Dunn, D. S., Smith, R. A., & Beins, B. C. (2007). *Best practices for teaching statistics and research methods for the behavioral sciences.* Mahwah, NJ: Erlbaum.

Dunn, D. S., Wilson, J. H., Freeman, J., & Stowell, J. R. (Eds.). (2011). *Best practices for technology-enhanced teaching & learning: Connecting to psychology and the social sciences.* New York, NY: Oxford University Press.

Dunn, D. S., Wilson, J. H., Gurung, R. A. R., & Naufel, K. (Eds.). (in press). *Hot topics: Best practices in teaching controversial issues in psychology.* Washington, DC: American Psychological Association.

Fried, C. B. (2008). In-class laptop use and its effects on student learning. *Computers & Education, 50,* 906–914. doi:10.1016/j.compedu.2006.09.006

Glassick, C. E., Huber, M. T., & Maeroff, G. I. (1997). *Scholarship assessed: Evaluation of the professoriate.* San Francisco, CA: Jossey-Bass.

Gurung, R. A. R. (2012). Consuming scholarship of teaching and learning: Using evidence-based pedagogy ethically. In R. E. Landrum & M. A. McCarthy (Eds.), *Teaching ethically: Challenges and opportunities* (pp. 67–76). Washington, DC: American Psychological Association.

Gurung, R. A. R., Ansburg, P. I., Alexander, P. A., Lawrence, N. K., & Johnson, D. E. (2008). The state of the scholarship of teaching and learning in psychology. *Teaching of Psychology, 35,* 249–261. doi:10.1080/00986280802374203

Gurung, R. A. R., & Prieto, L. R. (2009). *Getting culture: Incorporating diversity across the curriculum*. Sterling, VA: Stylus.

Gurung, R. A. R., & Schwartz, B. M. (2009). *Optimizing teaching and learning: Practicing pedagogical research*. Malden, MA: Wiley-Blackwell.

Gurung, R. A. R., & Schwartz, B. M. (2010). Riding the third wave of SoTL. *International Journal for the Scholarship of Teaching and Learning, 4*(2). Retrieved from http://academics.georgiasouthern.edu/ijsotl/v4n2/invited_essays/_GurungSchwartz/index.html

Gurung, R. A. R., & Vespia, K. M. (2007). Looking good, teaching well? Linking liking, looks, and learning. *Teaching of Psychology, 34*, 5–10.

Halpern, D. F., Smothergill, D. W., Allen, M., Baker, S., Baum, C., Best, D., . . . Weaver, K. A. (1998). Scholarship in psychology: A paradigm for the twenty-first century. *American Psychologist, 53*, 1292–1297. doi:10.1037/0003-066X.53.12.1292

Huber, M. T., & Hutchings, P. (2005). *The advancement of learning: Building the teaching commons*. San Francisco, CA: Jossey-Bass.

Hutchings, P., & Shulman, L. (1999). The scholarship of teaching: New elaborations, new developments. *Change, 31*(5), 10–15. Retrieved from http://www.carnegiefoundation.org/elibrary/scholarship-teaching-new-elaborations-new-developments

Irons, J. G., & Buskist, W. (2008). The scholarships of teaching and pedagogy: Time to abandon the distinction? *Teaching of Psychology, 35*, 353–356. doi:10.1080/00986280802373957

Melnyk, B. M., & Fineout-Overholt, E. (2005). *Evidence-based practice in nursing and healthcare: A guide to best practice*. Philadelphia, PA: Lippincott Williams & Wilkins.

Pan, D. (2009). What scholarship of teaching? Why bother? *International Journal for the Scholarship of Teaching and Learning, 3*(1). Retrieved from http://academics.georgiasouthern.edu/ijsotl/v3n1/invited_essays/_Pan/index.htm

Richlin, L. (2001). Scholarly teaching and the scholarship of teaching. In C. Kreber (Ed.), *Scholarship revisited: Perspectives on the scholarship of teaching* (pp. 57–68). San Francisco, CA: Jossey-Bass.

Smith, R. A. (2008). Moving toward the scholarship of teaching and learning: The classroom can be a lab, too! *Teaching of Psychology, 35*, 262–266. doi:10.1080/00986280802418711

Tomcho, T. J., & Foels, R. (2008). Assessing effective teaching of psychology: A meta-analytic integration of learning outcomes. *Teaching of Psychology, 35*, 286–296. doi:10.1080/00986280802374575

# 2

# BUILDING RAPPORT
# IN THE CLASSROOM AND
# STUDENT OUTCOMES

JANIE H. WILSON, SHAUNA B. WILSON,
AND ANGELA M. LEGG

Student–teacher rapport is considered to be one of the hallmarks of master teachers (Bain, 2004; Buskist, Sikorski, Buckley, & Saville, 2002; Keeley, Furr, & Buskist, 2009; Svinicki & McKeachie, 2011) and relates to better student attitudes as well as increased student motivation and grades (e.g., Wilson, Ryan, & Pugh, 2010). Research has primarily focused on rapport established and maintained during an ongoing term; however, even during course preparation prior to the first day of class, teachers can design policies that build rapport while still functioning within the limits of the course guidelines. In this chapter, we define rapport and present empirical evidence illustrating its importance in fostering positive student outcomes. We also discuss ways to build rapport both before and during a course and areas in need of further research.

## DEFINING AND MEASURING RAPPORT

The term *rapport* captures the positive relationship between instructor and students; Altman (1990) defined rapport to include interactions characterized by friendliness and caring. Traditionally, empirical literature has touched on the

23

construct using the term *immediacy*, defined as psychological availability that may or may not include physical proximity (Mehrabian, 1969). Although rapport is a larger construct than immediacy (Wilson et al., 2010), decades of immediacy research provide insight into specific behaviors that build positive relationships with students (e.g., Andersen, 1979). Many researchers have used the immediacy scale to measure the construct of immediacy. Items on this scale illustrate how immediacy can be divided into two components: verbal and nonverbal behaviors (Gorham & Christophel, 1990). Verbal behaviors rely on words such as *we* or *us* to build cohesion; nonverbal behaviors include smiling and making eye contact. Although at least one study suggested that nonverbal and verbal items represent only one factor (Gorham, 1988), the majority of immediacy research separates nonverbal and verbal items into separate measures (e.g., Frymier, 1993; Menzel & Carrell, 1999; Moore, Masterson, Christophel, & Shea, 1996).

Results from survey research have indicated that instructor verbal immediacy correlates with student motivation (Frymier, 1993; Wilson, 2006), perceptions of learning (Menzel & Carrell, 1999; Witt, Wheeless, & Allen, 2004), and attitude toward both the course and the instructor (Moore et al., 1996; Wilson, 2006). Similarly, nonverbal immediacy predicts student outcomes, including motivation (Christophel, 1990; Christophel & Gorham, 1995; Christensen & Menzel, 1998; Frymier, 1993), perceptions of learning (Christensen & Menzel, 1998; Witt et al., 2004), and attitude toward both the course and the instructor (Andersen, 1979; Andersen, Norton, & Nussbaum, 1981; Christensen & Menzel, 1998). Other research has suggested that the immediacy scale represents more than two factors, including three verbal components and one nonverbal component that help to predict student outcomes (Wilson & Locker, 2008).

One potentially useful nonverbal behavior not mentioned on the immediacy scale is touch. Mehrabian (1969) originally proposed five non-verbal immediacy cues: body orientation, eye contact, forward lean, distance, and touch. Touch is controversial in that it can be used inappropriately and can communicate various messages; however, appropriate touch may indeed communicate immediacy. In fact, Richmond, McCroskey, and Johnson (2003) argued that touch is an important way to establish rapport and that it should be returned to the immediacy scale.

In France, a male professor touching the forearms of students during a statistics exercise resulted in increased class participation (Guéguen, 2004). However, France is a relatively high-contact culture compared with the United States, which may limit generalizability. In one American sample of college students, Steward and Lupfer (1987) found evidence that touch enhanced perceptions of an instructor's effectiveness, and students who were touched earned higher grades on the subsequent course exam. In a more recent study, Wilson, Stadler, Schwartz, and Goff (2009) shook hands with half of their students on the first day of class. With a female instructor, students who shook hands rated her as more skillful in teaching and more likely to motivate students. With a male instructor, students who shook hands rated the professor as less skillful and less motivating. It should be noted that students' cultural background may affect their level of comfort with touch.

With the inclusion of touch in the immediacy literature, teachers have several behaviors from which to choose to communicate psychological availability. In order to remove the narrow limits of the immediacy scale, Wilson et al. (2010) created a scale to measure the more general construct of rapport in teaching. The rapport scale predicted unique portions of variance in instructor ratings beyond immediacy measures, with changes in $R^2$ ranging from 9% to 27%. Thus, creating rapport in the classroom seems based on students' general impressions of their professors. If teachers communicate a positive attitude toward students, students are likely to assume many other positive teaching qualities (Rosenberg, Nelson, & Vivekananthan, 1968), and their attitudes, motivation, and even grades are enhanced. A rapport scale that includes a number of perceptions related to student outcomes allows teachers to choose from a wealth of approaches to indicate concern for students without a restriction to potentially insincere behaviors. If smiling and calling students by name is uncomfortable for teachers, they can instead spend individual time with students helping them craft a superior paper. A focus on creating positive impressions with students encourages any behavior that genuinely communicates caring.

Although a plethora of immediacy literature exists, researchers should continue to examine newer elements of nonverbal immediacy, such as physically touching students. Simple surveys assessing student opinions of professor touch are likely to send the message that "touch is bad," but the same students who rate professor touch as negative are the students who seem to respond more positively to a professor after she has touched them (Wilson, Wilson, & North, 2009). A fruitful area of research may grow from the professor–student rapport scale that is now available (Wilson et al., 2010) and validated (R. G. Ryan, Wilson, & Pugh, 2011). Future studies may examine potential iterations of the scale with fewer items as well as tests of generalization to various teaching environments, such as online classes and other technologies, including Facebook.

## RAPPORT: FIRST IMPRESSIONS

The power of first impressions leads us to believe that student–teacher rapport should be established during our first interaction with students, regardless of the form of the first interaction (e.g., electronic or face-to-face).

Ambady and Rosenthal (1993) presented evidence that ratings of silent, 30-second video clips of teaching predicted end-of-semester student evaluations of professors. In fact, uncontrollable variables such as professor gender, age, and attractiveness affect the types of impressions students quickly form about their instructors (e.g., Berrenberg, 1987; Eagly, Ashmore, Makhijani, & Longo, 1991; Heilman & Stopeck, 1985; Lyons, 1981; Menzel & Carrell, 1999), and positive impressions (e.g., liking the professor) have been tied to self-reported student learning (Gurung & Vespia, 2007). But professors can overcome judgments that are based on uncontrollable factors before students even see them. Kelley (1950) found that students rated an unseen professor more favorably when a confederate described the professor as a "warm" rather than a "cold" person. Given existing technology, many opportunities exist for instructors to form positive first impressions and begin establishing rapport even before the first day of class.

Technologies such as WebCT, Blackboard, and e-mail afford instructors easy ways to communicate immediacy and build rapport before the official semester begins. Legg and Wilson (2009) demonstrated that a simple welcoming e-mail sent a week prior to the first day of class was sufficient to improve students' attitudes above a comparison group that did not receive an e-mail. At the first class meeting, students who had received the welcoming e-mail believed the instructor to be an excellent and effective teacher, reported more motivation toward the class, and would recommend the instructor to friends. Students even viewed the instructor as more prepared and able to present material more clearly. Finally, the e-mailed students reported a more positive attitude toward the course overall. Long-term benefits of this simple welcoming e-mail continued for female students at the midpoint and end of the semester. Female students reported higher motivation and evaluated the professor more favorably on preparedness and the amount of concern the instructor showed for students. In fact, retention was significantly better among students who received the welcoming e-mail relative to students who did not. Although grades did not differ, results indicated that teachers can build rapport even before a class begins by sending a simple welcoming e-mail.

Jacobson (1999) also demonstrated that positive first impressions can be formed before the first class meeting. He interviewed individuals from online social communities regarding the impressions formed about others they met online and how those impressions affect their face-to-face meetings. Jacobson concluded that people form impressions of others through computer-mediated communication, and these impressions carry over into face-to-face interactions. Thus, an added benefit of electronic communication (e.g., e-mail) is the absence of information that might activate stereotypes that are based on personal characteristics such as ethnicity and attractiveness. Students can form impressions that enhance rapport and are unclouded by face-to-face variables associated with first impressions.

It is clear that communicating with students before class begins is a low-maintenance, quick way for instructors to begin developing rapport with their students; however, a positive first day of class also is crucial. To determine empirically what students consider a "good" first day, Perlman and McCann (1999) asked students to compile a list of the most useful things a teacher can do on the first day as well as a list of first-day pet peeves. Results indicated that the most preferred first day included syllabus review, explanation of expectations and how to earn a good grade in the course, a short introduction of the teacher's background and teaching style, and a supportive and accessible attitude toward students. The most annoying first-day activities cited were poor use of class time (e.g., teacher being unprepared, providing unimportant information, reading the syllabus aloud), lecturing on course material, poor overview of the course, using the entire class period, assigning homework, and displaying an uncaring attitude toward students (see also Henslee, Burgess, & Buskist, 2006). These empirical data indicate what students prefer, but the potential impact of student preferences on outcomes such as motivation and learning remains relatively unexplored.

To empirically test whether the first day "matters" in terms of student outcomes, Wilson and Wilson (2007) examined students' motivation, course rating, perceived effectiveness of the professor, attitude toward the professor, and grades in the course. Students experienced a first day based on student preferences or a first day based on expert teaching opinion. Students who received a first day based on expert suggestions stayed the entire class period, received a homework assignment, and saw the professor go over the syllabus in a no-nonsense manner (e.g., formal presentation style without smiling). Students who experienced a first day based on student preferences saw the professor cover the syllabus in a friendly manner (e.g., smiling), did not receive a homework assignment, and left class early. Results indicated that students who had the student-friendly first-day experience remained more motivated across the term than did those with the first day based on the advice of teaching experts. Additionally, scores on the final exam were significantly higher for those who experienced the student-friendly first day.

As a second indication that early impressions in the classroom impact students, Hermann, Foster, and Hardin (2010) examined a reciprocal-interview activity. During the first week of classes, several instructors allowed students in small groups to prepare interview questions to be used when interviewing the instructor in front of the class; a second group of instructors did not use the technique. Interview questions pertained to course goals, classroom norms, and supportive instructor behaviors. Students of instructors who used the reciprocal-interview exercise at the beginning of the term reported higher satisfaction with the course, more clarity about what was required of them, and greater support from the instructor at the end of the term. These findings indicate that we the need to go beyond expert advice and illustrate the need to empirically test what is thought to provide best practices in the classroom.

Given the previously discussed findings, we suggest that the first days should include covering the syllabus and course expectations, conveying a supportive and caring attitude toward students (perhaps by using the reciprocal-interview technique), and refraining from jumping too quickly into course material and homework assignments. Although teachers should display authentic immediacy throughout the semester, care should be taken on the first days in particular, as it may set the tone for the remainder of the term.

At this point, teachers do not know exactly which aspects of a positive first day enhance motivation and grades, opening teaching scholarship to numerous additional questions. Further, if teachers decide to make their first contact with students prior to the first day via e-mail, researchers need to examine the best content and timing for the e-mail and whether more than one welcoming e-mail should be sent.

## POTENTIAL CLASSROOM CHALLENGES TO RAPPORT

As a term unfolds, course obligations can wreak havoc on rapport. Teachers regularly demand performance from their students, which is rife with potential for conflict. Teachers must (a) require students to perform, (b) set deadlines, (c) provide feedback on student work, and (d) reflect less-than-perfect work by giving grades lower than 100%. If teachers hope to maintain rapport across an entire course, it is crucial to identify ways to avoid conflict and recognize the vast power differential between teacher and student. If they fail to consider potential pitfalls throughout the term, rapport based on positive first impressions may be lost. However, teachers can plan ahead and set course policies that protect positive relationships with students.

### The Social Classroom

Novotney (2010) suggested that instructors should take a more informal approach to teaching, being more relaxed, accessible, and approachable than perhaps professors of a prior age. According to Novotney, today's college students have closer relationships with their parents and other adults, which may explain why teacher self-disclosure (e.g., using personal examples) connected with course content relates to student learning and motivation (Cayanus & Martin, 2008). Perhaps students expect teachers to be accessible enough to connect with them on a more personal level. Along these same lines, students want to be called by name (e.g., Gorham, 1988; Wilson & Taylor, 2001). We maintain that bonding with students is crucial, but being "friendly" with students does not indicate being "friends" with students. Friendliness connotes kindness toward students and a willingness to spend time helping them succeed in class, whereas friendship includes sharing personal confidences and favors in an equal relationship (see Wilson, Smalley, &Yancey [2012] for a discussion of ethical boundaries when building rapport with students). Maintaining a friendly bond with students can become a challenge when teachers dive into course-management details such as testing and quizzing, reviewing papers, assigning homework, and engaging in out-of-class communications.

## Tests and Quizzes

Testing is arguably one of the most anxiety-provoking course experiences for students. Professors should strive to create their tests and the testing environment such that rapport remains intact, although empirical examination of classroom testing is in short supply.

Students often complain about unfair tests and grading procedures or unexpected material appearing on examinations (Brown & Tomlin, 1996). When grading tests, teachers can recognize that perfect questions are rare. One policy to circumvent arguments with students is to drop a few questions from a test; for example, an instructor could credit back the equivalent of three items on a 50-item multiple-choice test. A second strategy allows students to receive their test and take 5 minutes to write a rationale for a specific grade change, offering support from their textbook and notes. The instructor can review the rationale and respond to the student in writing at the end of the next class period. Whenever possible, teachers should avoid unpleasantness with the class when going over a test.

Similar to testing, quizzing can influence student–teacher rapport. To enhance learning, professors ask students to study material outside of the classroom. Poor class preparation on the part of the students is a bone of contention for many teachers and can readily damage rapport. However, teacher–scholars know that ongoing preparation (distributed practice) enhances learning beyond bingeing on course information immediately before a test (massed practice; Dempster, 1988).

One way to encourage student preparation is to have unannounced quizzes, which may increase test grades by encouraging distributed practice of the material (Graham, 1999). Unfortunately, teachers who use unannounced quizzes know the potential damage to rapport. Students scramble to look over notes, grumble to each other, or even express outright indignation. However, Graham revealed a positive attitude toward quizzing by students, with the vast majority rating the quizzes as a good idea for the course and a practice that would benefit other courses. On the basis of such positive ratings, we suggest maintaining rapport while quizzing by (a) letting students know on the first day of class and on the syllabus that they will take frequent unannounced quizzes; (b) explaining Graham's results of higher grades as well as Roediger's research on repeated testing as an excellent way to learn material (e.g., Roediger & Karpicke, 2006); (c) on a quiz day, announcing that students will have the opportunity to improve their grades today; (d) dropping the lowest quiz grade at the end of the term; or (e) using quizzes as bonus points for upcoming tests.

In this section, we have outlined numerous areas in need of study. The opinions of experienced teachers offer a good starting point from which to craft research questions, but data must shed light on the most useful testing and quizzing policies.

**Papers**

In addition to tests and quizzes, instructors evaluate student writing. As a threat to rapport, a recurrent problem with student papers is plagiarism. One way to discourage students from plagiarizing others' written work is to use a plagiarism-detection website such as turnitin (http://www. turnitin.com). This website allows for anonymous comparison of students' written work with websites, books, journals, and periodicals as well as with the website's store of previously submitted student work. Dahl (2007) found that students generally react positively toward professors using turnitin, citing that students are "happy" that this system makes plagiarism more difficult. Only a small subsample of students expressed concern with turnitin, and concern may have been due to their self-reported inability to correctly quote references. Perhaps when turnitin is used, students will be less likely to cheat on their papers, and awkward confrontations that might damage rapport may be reduced. However, this idea awaits empirical investigation.

An alternative for reducing academically dishonest behavior is the use of an honor code. Although not all institutions have an honor system, instructors can include one in any course. When an instructor includes an honor code and discusses how it applies to assignments and exams, students more clearly understand what is defined as academically dishonest behavior and in turn are less likely to act dishonestly when it comes to academic work for that course (McCabe & Trevino, 1993). Of course, instructors need to clearly communicate to students how the honor code applies within a course and also to discuss with students the importance of academic integrity (Schwartz, Tatum, & Wells, 2012).

## Homework

The completion of homework predicts student confidence in course material, cognitive learning, and quiz grades. Developing policies for homework would seem to be an important step in creating a positive classroom climate. Assigning too much homework could make the instructor appear authoritarian or uncaring about students' other out-of-class responsibilities. In fact, assignment overload tops the list of precursors to student burnout (Cushman & West, 2006). Assigning too little homework results in disadvantages as well, such as fewer opportunities for students to receive feedback about their progress in the course.

To gain the potential advantages of homework without overwhelming and alienating students, researchers can examine the following strategies: assign a reasonable amount of homework, provide reasons why students should complete homework, and provide quick and thorough feedback on assignments. Slow turnaround time for grading and returning work ranked fifth on a student-created list of instructor misbehaviors (Kearney, Plax, Hays, & Ivey, 1991). In addition, homework should impact grades. C. S. Ryan and Hemmes (2005) found that students who earned grades for completed homework assignments made higher scores on subsequent quizzes compared with students who did not receive grades for homework. Additionally, homework assignments were less likely to be turned in if no grade was offered. Finally, teachers should avoid accepting late homework. This practice is unfair to students who turn in work on time.

## Out-of-Class Communication

Out-of-class communication (OCC) benefits both students and instructors by fostering positive student attitudes (e.g., Myers, 2004). Beyond the traditional ways in which instructors can interact with students (e.g., office hours), students can also use technology such as e-mail, social networking sites, and online-chat programs to interact with their instructors beyond classroom time. However, the ethical implications of OCC are important to consider. Instructors should establish policies for OCC to govern their behaviors, and the utility of policies ultimately should be assessed. Hevern (2006) argued that messages sent through online media are easily misconstrued because there are no nonverbal or other contextual cues. For example, e-mails can convey irritation with a student when teachers might simply have been in a hurry when typing. As an added dimension, any negative emotion implicit in an e-mail lasts forever; the message can be forwarded to others, saved, or printed in a hard copy. We suggest that teachers might enjoy the benefits of building rapport through positive e-mails and should carefully word any e-mails that could possibly be perceived as negative. The best approach to e-mailing students remains to be illustrated by research.

In addition to the potential benefits of e-mail communications, student–teacher interactions through social networking sites such as Facebook (http://www.facebook.com/) may affect rapport (Mazer, Murphy, & Simonds, 2007, 2009). Mazer and colleagues (2009) manipulated instructor self-disclosure on a Facebook profile and asked student participants to view the profile and rate the potential instructors with low, medium, or high levels of self-disclosure. Participants reported more motivation and more positive attitudes toward the instructor in the high self-disclosure condition. Using a similar methodology, Mazer et al. (2009) reported increased perceptions of credibility for the instructor in the high self-disclosure condition. Thus, instructors who self-disclose on Facebook may enjoy positive student perceptions and higher student motivation. However, it is important to note that such self-disclosure with students in social media raises ethical concerns, such as the possibility of dual relationships with students. Additionally, students in the Mazer et al. (2009) study noted that instructors could present themselves in an unprofessional way. Specifically, students suggested that instructors not provide details about political orientations and monitor comments allowed on the public wall. Further advice concerning fair and ethical treatment of students also emerged as a popular concern among students. Participants warned instructors against gossiping and spying on students and asked that instructors respect students' privacy.

Taken together, evidence has suggested that online interactions with students may enhance rapport, but interactions must be professional and respectful and care must be taken to avoid ethical problems. Until more research becomes available, professors should develop policies when navigating online student–instructor affiliations. By forming well-thought-out policies concerning social networking site interaction, instructors can proactively navigate the many ethical concerns related to this new form of instructor–student interaction. In the end, assessment of online interactions is crucial.


## CONCLUSION

In this chapter, we have discussed student–teacher rapport, including enhanced student attitudes toward the teacher and the course as well as higher student motivation, perceived learning, and grades. Exhibits 2.1 and 2.2 summarize the best practices to enhance rapport and future directions for the scholarship of teaching and learning (SoTL) on this topic. Although most teachers (as well as teaching publications) focus on grades as the primary concern, we would argue that student attitudes and motivation to succeed in class are tied to learning, and grades are only one measure of learning. In

EXHIBIT 2.1
Evidence-Based Recommendations

- Send a welcoming e-mail to students before the first day of class.
- Provide students with a positive first day of class.
- Avoid icebreakers on Day 1 of class.
- Use unannounced quizzes to encourage learning without compromising rapport.
- Assess plagiarism by using online programs without jeopardizing rapport.
- Grade and return homework quickly.
- Send positive communications to students via electronic media.

fact, correlations among student attitudes, motivation, and learning have been established, with learning defined as students' self-reports of grades at the end of the term (Wilson, 2006). Teacher–scholars must decide whether establishing and maintaining rapport with students is worth the effort if the only assessed outcomes have been higher motivation and more positive student attitudes. On the basis of links between motivation, student attitudes, and learning, the answer would seem to be yes.

Researchers interested in SoTL can focus their attention on empirically testing the validity of expert opinion. Areas ripe for student–teacher rapport research were included throughout this chapter and include (a) the influence of teacher immediacy behaviors such as touch, (b) the many possible ways to foster positive first impressions through electronic contact or meeting on the first day of class, and (c) course policies that help teachers manage classes without destroying rapport. Teaching has reached an exciting point: Teacher–scholars empirically examine what actually enhances student attitudes, motivation, and learning. In these early stages of research, a great deal remains to be accomplished in SoTL.

EXHIBIT 2.2
Questions for Future Research

- What is the role of appropriate professor touch when building rapport?
- What content, timing, and number of e-mails should be used?
- Which aspects of a positive first day matter the most (e.g., being friendly, covering only the syllabus, allowing students to leave early)?
- How can teachers get to know students while avoiding mindless icebreakers?
- Which aspects of testing or quizzing enhance learning and salvage rapport?
- With improved student–teacher rapport, are students less likely to cheat? Do professors have fewer confrontations with students?
- Does a professor compromise rapport by accepting late work?
- What aspects of communication or type of media affect rapport? Should bad news always be given in person?
- How much self-disclosure and what topics of disclosure build rapport? Is this effect moderated by type of teacher, discipline, or even teacher age?

# REFERENCES

Altman, I. (1990). Conceptualizing "rapport." *Psychological Inquiry, 1,* 294–323. doi:10.1207/s15327965pli0104_2

Ambady, N., & Rosenthal, R. (1993). Half a minute: Predicting teacher evaluations from thin slices of nonverbal behavior and physical attractiveness. *Journal of Personality and Social Psychology, 64,* 431–441. doi:10.1037/0022-3514.64.3.431

Andersen, J. F. (1979). Teacher immediacy as a predictor of teaching effectiveness. In D. Nimmo (Ed.), *Communication yearbook 3* (pp. 543–559). New Brunswick, NJ: Transaction Books.

Andersen, J. F., Norton, R. W., & Nussbaum, J. F. (1981). Three investigations exploring relationships between perceived teacher communication behaviors and student learning. *Communication Education, 30,* 377–392. doi:10.1080/03634528109378493

Bain, K. (2004). *What the best college teachers do.* Cambridge, MA: Harvard University Press.

Berrenberg, J. L. (1987). A classroom exercise in impression formation. *Teaching of Psychology, 14,* 169–170. doi:10.1207/s15328023top1403_10

Brown, W., & Tomlin, J. (1996). Best and worst university teachers: The opinions of undergraduate students. *College Student Journal, 30,* 431–434.

Buskist, W., Sikorski, J., Buckley, T., & Saville, B. K. (2002). Elements of master teaching. In S. F. Davis & W. Buskist (Eds.), *The teaching of psychology: Essays in honor of Wilbert J. McKeachie and Charles L. Brewer* (pp. 27–39). Mahwah, NJ: Erlbaum.

Cayanus, J. L., & Martin, M. M. (2008). Teacher self-disclosure: Amount, relevance, and negativity. *Communication Quarterly, 56,* 325–341. doi:10.1080/01463370802241492

Christensen, L. J., & Menzel, K. E. (1998). The linear relationship between student reports of teacher immediacy behaviors and perceptions of state motivation, and of cognitive, affective, and behavioral learning. *Communication Education, 47,* 82–90. doi:10.1080/03634529809379112

Christophel, D. M. (1990). The relationships among teacher immediacy behaviors, student motivation, and learning. *Communication Education, 39,* 323–340. doi:10.1080/03634529009378813

Christophel, D. M., & Gorham, J. (1995). A test-retest analysis of student motivation, teacher immediacy, and perceived sources of motivation and demotivation in college classes. *Communication Education, 44,* 292–306. doi:10.1080/03634529509379020

Cushman, S., & West, R. (2006). Precursors to college student burnout: Developing a typology of understanding. *Qualitative Research Reports in Communication, 7,* 23–31. doi:10.1080/17459430600964638

Dahl, S. (2007). Turnitin®: The student perspective on using plagiarism detection software. *Active Learning in Higher Education, 8,* 173–191. doi:10.1177/1469787407074110

Dempster, F. N. (1988). The spacing effect: A case study in the failure to apply the results of psychological research. *American Psychologist, 43,* 627–634. doi:10.1037/0003-066X.43.8.627

Eagly, A. H., Ashmore, R. D., Makhijani, M. G., & Longo, L. C. (1991). What is beautiful is good, but . . . : A meta-analytic review of research on the physical attractiveness stereotype. *Psychological Bulletin, 110,* 109–128. doi:10.1037/0033-2909.110.1.109

Frymier, A. B. (1993). The relationships among communication apprehension, immediacy and motivation to study. *Communication Reports, 6,* 8–17. doi:10.1080/08934219309367556

Gorham, J. (1988). The relationship between verbal teacher immediacy behaviors and student learning. *Communication Education, 37,* 40–53. doi:10.1080/03634528809378702

Gorham, J., & Christophel, D. M. (1990). The relationship of teachers' use of humor in the classroom to immediacy and student learning. *Communication Education, 39,* 46–62. doi:10.1080/03634529009378786

Graham, R. B. (1999). Unannounced quizzes raise test scores selectively for mid-range students. *Teaching of Psychology, 26,* 271–273. doi:10.1207/S15328023 TOP260406

Guéguen, N. (2004). Nonverbal encouragement of participation in a course: The effect of touching. *Social Psychology of Education, 7,* 89–98. doi:10.1023/B:SPOE.0000010691.30834.14

Gurung, R. A. R., & Vespia, K. M. (2007). Looking good, teaching well? Linking liking, good looks, and learning. *Teaching of Psychology, 34,* 5–10.

Heilman, M. E., & Stopeck, M. H. (1985). Being attractive, advantage or disadvantage? Performance-based evaluations and recommended personnel actions as a function of appearance, sex, and job type. *Organizational Behavior and Human Decision Processes, 35,* 202–215. doi:10.1016/0749-5978(85)90035-4

Henslee, A. M., Burgess, D. R., & Buskist, W. (2006). Students' preferences for first day of class activities. *Teaching of Psychology, 33,* 189–191. doi:10.1207/s15328023top3303_7

Hermann, A. D., Foster, D. A., & Hardin, E. E. (2010). Does the first week of class matter? A quasi-experimental investigation of student satisfaction. *Teaching of Psychology, 37,* 79–84. doi:10.1080/00986281003609314

Hevern, V. W. (2006). Using the Internet effectively: Homepages and e-mail. In W. Buskist & S. F. Davis (Eds.), *Handbook of the teaching of psychology* (pp. 99–106). Malden, MA: Blackwell. doi:10.1002/9780470754924.ch17

Jacobson, D. (1999). Impression formation in cyberspace: Online expectations and offline experiences in text-based virtual communities. *Journal of Computer-Mediated Communication, 5*(1). Retrieved from http://jcmc,indiana.edu/vol5/issue1/jacobson.html

Kearney, P., Plax, T. G., Hays, E. R., & Ivey, M. J. (1991). College teacher misbehaviors: What students don't like about what teachers say and do. *Communication Quarterly, 39,* 309–324. doi:10.1080/01463379109369808

Keeley, J., Furr, M. R., & Buskist, W. (2009). Differentiating psychology students' perceptions of teachers using the teacher behavior checklist. *Teaching of Psychology, 37*, 16–20. doi:10.1080/00986280903426282

Kelley, H. H. (1950). The warm-cold variable in first impressions of persons. *Journal of Personality, 18*, 431–439. doi:10.1111/j.1467-6494.1950.tb01260.x

Legg, A. M., & Wilson, J. H. (2009). E-mail from professor enhances student motivation and attitudes. *Teaching of Psychology, 36*, 205–211. doi:10.1080/00986280902960034

Lyons, A. (1981). Introducing students to social psychology through student-generated first impressions of the professor. *Teaching of Psychology, 8*, 173–174. doi:10.1207/s15328023top0803_16

Mazer, J. P., Murphy, R. E., & Simonds, C. J. (2007). I'll see you on "Facebook": The effects of computer-mediated teacher self-disclosure on student motivation, affective learning, and classroom climate. *Communication Education, 56*, 1–17. doi:10.1080/03634520601009710

Mazer, J. P., Murphy, R. E., & Simonds, C. J. (2009). The effects of teacher self-disclosure via Facebook on teacher credibility. *Learning, Media and Technology, 34*, 175–183. doi:10.1080/17439880902923655

McCabe, D. L., & Trevino, L. K. (1993). Academic dishonesty: Honor codes and other contextual influences. *The Journal of Higher Education, 64*, 522–538. doi:10.2307/2959991

Mehrabian, A. (1969). Some referents and measures of nonverbal behavior. *Behavior Research Methods and Instrumentation, 1*, 203–207. doi:10.3758/BF03208096

Menzel, K. E., & Carrell, L. J. (1999). The impact of gender and immediacy on willingness to talk and perceived learning. *Communication Education, 48*, 31–40. doi:10.1080/03634529909379150

Moore, A., Masterson, J. T., Christophel, D. M., & Shea, K. A. (1996). College teacher immediacy and student ratings of instruction. *Communication Education, 45*, 29–39. doi:10.1080/03634529609379030

Myers, S. A. (2004). The relationship between perceived instructor credibility and college student out-of-class communication. *Communication Reports, 17*, 129–137. doi:10.1080/08934210409389382

Novotney, A. (2010). Engaging the millennial learner. *Monitor on Psychology, 41*, 60–62.

Perlman, B., & McCann, L. I. (1999). Student perspectives on the first day of class. *Teaching of Psychology, 26*, 277–279. doi:10.1207/S15328023TOP260408

Richmond, V. P., McCroskey, J. C., & Johnson, A. D. (2003). Development of the nonverbal immediacy scale (NIS): Measures of self- and other-perceived nonverbal immediacy. *Communication Quarterly, 51*, 504–517. doi:10.1080/01463370309370170

Roediger, H. L., & Karpicke, J. D. (2006). Test-enhanced learning. *Psychological Science, 17*, 249–255. doi:10.1111/j.1467-9280.2006.01693.x

Rosenberg, S., Nelson, S., & Vivekananthan, P. S. (1968). A multidimensional approach to the structure of personality impressions. *Journal of Personality and Social Psychology, 9*, 283–294. doi:10.1037/h0026086

Ryan, C. S., & Hemmes, N. S. (2005). Effects of the contingency for homework submission on homework submission and quiz performance in a college course. *Journal of Applied Behavior Analysis, 38,* 79–88. doi:10.1901/jaba.2005.123-03

Ryan, R. G., Wilson, J. H., & Pugh, J. L. (2011). Psychometric properties of the professor-student rapport scale. *Teaching of Psychology, 38,* 135–141.

Schwartz, B. M., Tatum, H. E., & Wells, J. W. (2012). The honor code: Influences on attitudes, behaviors, and pedagogy. In R. E. Landrum & M. A. McCarthy (Eds.), *Teaching ethically: Challenges and opportunities* (pp. 89–98). Washington, DC: American Psychological Association.

Steward, A. L., & Lupfer, M. (1987). Touching as teaching: The effect of touch on students' perceptions and performance. *Journal of Applied Social Psychology, 17,* 800–809. doi:10.1111/j.1559-1816.1987.tb00340.x

Svinicki, M., & McKeachie, W. J. (2011). *McKeachie's teaching tips.* Belmont, CA: Wadsworth.

Wilson, J. H. (2006). Predicting student attitudes and grades from perceptions of instructors' attitudes. *Teaching of Psychology, 33,* 91–95. doi:10.1207/s15328023 top3302_2

Wilson, J. H., & Locker, L. (2008). Immediacy scale represents four factors: Non-verbal and verbal components predict student outcomes. *Journal of Classroom Interaction, 42,* 4–10.

Wilson, J. H., Ryan, R. G., & Pugh, J. L. (2010). Professor-student rapport scale predicts student outcomes. *Teaching of Psychology, 37,* 246–251. doi:10.1080/00986283.2010.510976

Wilson, J. H., Smalley, K. B., & Yancey, C. T. (2012). Building Relationships With Students and Maintaining Ethical Boundaries. In R. E. Landrum & M. A. McCarthy (Eds.), *Teaching ethically: Challenges and opportunities* (pp.139–150). Washington, DC: American Psychological Association.

Wilson, J. H., Stadler, J. R., Schwartz, B. M., & Goff, D. M. (2009). Touching your students: The impact of a handshake on the first day of class. *Journal of the Scholarship of Teaching and Learning, 9,* 108–117. Retrieved from https://www.iupui.edu/josotl/archive/vol_9/no_1/v9n1wilson.pdf

Wilson, J. H., & Taylor, K. W. (2001). Professor immediacy as behaviors associated with liking students. *Teaching of Psychology, 28,* 136–138.

Wilson, J. H., & Wilson, S. B. (2007). The first day of class affects student motivation: An experimental study. *Teaching of Psychology, 34,* 226–230.

Wilson, J. H., Wilson, S. B., & North, E. L. (2009, May). *Professor touch may be detrimental.* Poster presented at the meeting of the Association for Psychological Science, San Francisco, CA.

Witt, P. L., Wheeless, L. R., & Allen, M. (2004). A meta-analytical review of the relationship between teacher immediacy and student learning. *Communication Monographs, 71,* 184–207. doi:10.1080/036452042000228054

# 3

# USING TECHNOLOGY TO ENHANCE
# TEACHING AND LEARNING

## CHRISTOPHER R. POIRIER AND ROBERT S. FELDMAN

Technology is changing undergraduate education as a number of innovative technologies have made their way into college classrooms in recent years (Millis et al., 2010). Although new technologies often show great promise, college instructors face significant challenges when adopting and implementing technology to facilitate good teaching. This chapter provides instructors with a critical examination of the research on using technology in the classroom so that their decisions about technology will be based on objective, empirical findings. We describe several popular technologies, including blogs, wikis, instant messaging, and social networking, and review the relevant scholarship of teaching and learning (SoTL) findings and the implications of incorporating the technology in the classroom. We also discuss suggestions for the best application of each technology and explore ideas for future SoTL.

## PRESENTATION SOFTWARE

Presentation software, such as Microsoft PowerPoint and Apple Keynote, has become a widely accepted teaching tool in higher education. Presentation software allows instructors to develop multimedia presentations containing text, graphics, audio clips, and video segments. Proponents of presentation software have argued that it helps speakers to organize ideas by forcing instructors to present their topic in a linear, logical fashion (Hlynka & Mason, 1998). Moreover, Apperson, Laws, and Scepansky (2006) found that the use of slideware presentations allowed students to stay focused on the lecture and increased their interest in the course material. Interestingly, the students also reported that they liked the professor more when PowerPoint was used.

But not everyone is positive about the use of presentation software. For instance, Tufte (2004) contended that PowerPoint simplifies content and suppresses creative thinking. Despite such criticisms, research has shown that if presentation software is used properly, it can improve learning (see Mayer & Moreno, 2003, for a review). Mayer and colleagues have proposed a theory of multimedia learning and published the results of dozens of experiments in support of the theory. According to the theory, the main challenge for instructors is trying to limit the learner's cognitive load. On the basis of their empirical work, Mayer and Moreno (2003) provided a number of suggestions for reducing cognitive load. For example, instructors should reduce on-screen text by presenting words as narration and divide longer presentations into bite-size segments. In addition, it is important to eliminate extraneous material (e.g., background music) and provide cues (e.g., headings, arrows) for what is essential content. Furthermore, when using both images and text, instructors should spatially align the images with the corresponding text. If instructors follow these theory-based suggestions, students should gain a deeper understanding of the material presented.

Research has revealed that students prefer PowerPoint lectures over traditional lectures (Bartsch & Cobern, 2003; Frey & Birnbaum, 2002; Susskind, 2005, 2008). However, in terms of students' learning outcomes, the research is mixed. Susskind (2008) compared students instructed with overhead transparencies with students instructed with PowerPoint presentations. He found that students preferred the PowerPoint lectures over the traditional lectures because the PowerPoint lectures were better organized, more interesting, and enjoyable. Although the students liked the PowerPoint lectures more, Susskind found that this teaching format did not have an effect on students' exam performance, attendance, and participation in class discussions. These findings are similar to previous research results on PowerPoint in which no changes in learning outcomes emerged (Apperson et al., 2006; DeBord, Aruguete, & Muhlig, 2004; Hardin, 2007; Susskind, 2005; Szabo & Hastings, 2000).

Despite many studies concluding that PowerPoint presentations do not affect learning, some studies have found small positive effects (Axtell, Maddux, & Aberasturi, 2008; Hove & Corcoran, 2008a). For instance, Hove and Corcoran (2008a) administered a multiple-choice pretest and then randomly assigned participants to one of three lecture conditions: traditional lecture, slide-show-supplemented lecture, and virtual learning environment (no face-to-face contact). Overall, Hove and Corcoran (2008a) found that the students in the slide-show-supplemented lecture and virtual learning conditions learned more than students in the traditional lecture condition. One likely explanation for the mixed results is that other critical factors are involved in the relationship between teaching with PowerPoint and student learning. For instance, Susskind (2005) found that multimedia slide show presentations enhanced students' self-efficacy. The students believed that the PowerPoint lectures were more organized, making it easier to take notes and study for tests. Other research has suggested that students' level of perceptual and attentional arousal may mediate the relationship (Hove & Corcoran, 2008a). Presentations consisting of both audio and video clips may produce greater arousal and motivate students to a greater degree, causing them to learn more. Of course, if presentations cause cognitive overload, students will likely learn less (Mayer & Moreno, 2003).

An issue related to the use of presentation software to supplement lectures is students' preference to have access to the slides before and after class on course websites. Some fear that students will be more likely to skip class if the slides are available. However, recent research has suggested that students with access to slides before class do not attend class less frequently (Babb & Ross, 2009; Bowman, 2009; Hove & Corcoran, 2008b). Another important concern relates to the consequences of access to PowerPoint slides prior to class on student learning. To test the effect of access to PowerPoint slides on learning, Hove and Corcoran (2008b) provided students in one section of introductory psychology with unlimited online access prior to and after class to all PowerPoint presentations. Students in a second section did not have access to the presentations, except during class. They found that students who had online access to the presentations earned significantly higher exam grades than students without access. Having access to the presentations online may have allowed students to keep up with the content when they missed class. These studies are tempered by others that show that access to lecture slides had no effect on learning outcomes (Bowman, 2009; Frank, Shaw, & Wilson, 2008–2009; Noppe, Achterberg, Duquaine, Huebbe, & Williams, 2007).

Another important factor to consider is the type of slides provided to the students. If instructors provide access to presentation slides, what should be included? Some instructors provide identical copies, but others provide broad outlines. Cornelius and Owen-DeSchryver (2008) found that students receiving instructor-provided partial notes performed better on a cumulative final exam than students receiving full notes. Barnett (2003) also investigated the use of providing notes and found that students who received complete lecture notes earned lower exam grades than students who received skeletal outline notes. Therefore, it appears that partial notes are better for students.

Although the effect of presentation software on students' learning has received considerable attention, future research is necessary to answer a number of key questions. In general, because most studies have relied on nonexperimental or quasi-experimental research designs (e.g., Apperson et al., 2006; Bowman, 2009; Frank et al., 2008–2009; Hardin, 2007; Hove & Corcoran, 2008b; Susskind, 2008), additional research relying on true experiments is necessary. In addition, it is difficult to evaluate and compare previous studies because researchers did not report what they added to their slides. On the basis of the research by Mayer and colleagues (e.g., Mayer & Moreno, 2003), it is important to closely examine the type of content (e.g., text, images) that instructors put on their slides, as well as any supplemental information they provide to their students. Furthermore, the characteristics of the instructor should not be overlooked when testing the effects of presentation software on student learning outcomes (see Hardin, 2007), and future work should examine how students' behaviors, including note taking and studying, are influenced by having access to presentations before and after class. Finally, because PowerPoint has been the focal point of most studies, additional research testing the effects of different software (e.g., Apple Keynote) is imperative (see Ludwig, Daniel, Froman, & Mathie, 2004, for a review of best practices).

## AUDIENCE RESPONSE SYSTEMS

An *audience response system* consists of a receiver connected to a computer and a set of remote personal keypads, commonly called *clickers*, which allow instructors to quickly collect feedback from students. To use the technology (e.g., TurningPoint by Turning Technologies, Classroom Performance System by eInstruction), instructors prepare multiple-choice questions in presentation software (e.g., PowerPoint). Then during class, the questions are displayed on a classroom projection screen, and each student responds by pressing a button on a clicker to communicate an answer. After students respond, the computer aggregates the responses and presents the results in a histogram. These data can be viewed and discussed by both students and instructor in real time. In addition, the data file can be saved for future use, and students' responses can be used for grading.

In general, students' attitudes toward using an audience response system are very positive (Hunsinger, Poirier, & Feldman, 2008; Patry, 2009; Pemberton, Borrego, & Cohen, 2006; Poirier & Feldman, 2007), and there are many potential benefits of using clickers. First, research has shown that using clickers changes the nature of classroom dynamics by increasing students' participation (Burnstein & Lederman, 2001; Hunsinger et al., 2008; Poirier & Feldman, 2007; Stowell & Nelson, 2007; Trees & Jackson, 2007). Second, because responses are anonymous to their peers (and can, if the instructor wishes, be made anonymous to the instructor), students can contribute without feeling judged (Draper & Brown, 2004; Stowell & Nelson, 2007; Stowell, Oldham, & Bennett, 2010). Third, students report that they are more likely to pay attention during classes that use clickers (Hoekstra, 2008; Hunsinger et al., 2008; Poirier & Feldman, 2007). Presenting questions at 20-minute intervals is optimal (see Kay & LeSage, 2009, for a review). Fourth, instructors can use the technology to acquire immediate feedback during the lecture, which may allow them to change the pace or reinforce a concept that students have not mastered, as evidenced by their clicker responses (Abrahamson, 2006; Hake, 1998).

Finally, and perhaps most important, several studies have shown that clickers increase learning (Crouch & Mazur, 2001; Kennedy & Cutts, 2005; Mayer et al., 2009; Morling, McAuliffe, Cohen, & DiLorenzo, 2008; Poirier & Feldman, 2007), although the evidence is not entirely consistent. For instance, Mayer et al. (2009) and Morling et al. (2008) found that students using clickers scored significantly higher on course exams than students who did not use clickers. On the other hand, some studies have not found evidence for an increase in quiz and exam scores (e.g., Christopherson, 2011; Pemberton et al., 2006; Stowell & Nelson, 2007). Major differences between the studies may have contributed to the different findings. For example, in the studies that did show an impact on student learning, instructors taught with clickers for the entire semester. In contrast, Pemberton et al. (2006) relied on the technology just for review sessions, and Stowell and Nelson (2007) examined a single 30-minute lecture. To incorporate clickers in a course, Caldwell (2007) and Kay and LeSage (2009) provided best practice tips.

Although the predominant evidence is that clickers can improve teaching and learning, there are potential drawbacks to their use. First, technical difficulties may disrupt lecture flow and cause frustration and anxiety (see Kay & LeSage, 2009). Second, students with limited technology experience may be anxious when audience response systems are first introduced (Beatty, 2004; Hoekstra, 2008). However, in a more recent study, Zapf and Garcia (2011) found that although students low in technology proficiency held less favorable views of clickers, they were more engaged and earned higher final course grades than students high in technology proficiency. Thus, less comfort with clickers may not lead to a decrease in learning (i.e., lower grades). Third, some students view the use of the technology as a waste of time (d'Inverno, Davis, & White, 2003; Hunsinger et al., 2008; Poirier & Feldman, 2007).

Finally, it is clear that writing effective questions is imperative. Although there are guidelines for creating effective questions (see Caldwell, 2007), it is a time-consuming task.

Although there is a substantial body of research on the use of audience response systems, several significant questions remain unanswered. For one, research is needed to examine the effects of additional factors related to the teaching and learning environment on the efficacy of using clickers. For instance, students' personality traits may moderate the relationship between clickers and learning outcomes (e.g., Hunsinger et al., 2008). Second, future research should explore the types of questions that are most effective for specific learning environments (Caldwell, 2007; Kay & LeSage, 2009). Finally, because nearly half of the studies on clickers are qualitative (Kay & LeSage, 2009), additional quantitative data are necessary, especially a finer grained analysis of the impact of clicker use on different sorts of learning outcomes.

## PODCASTING

Podcasts are systems of software and hardware that permit individuals to access audio and visual files. To create a lecture podcast, instructors can record all or part of a lecture by using microphones built into computers and lecture-capture technology, such as a system provided commercially by Tegrity (http://www.tegrity.com). Then, instructors provide students with access to the file. Some instructors offer synchronized e-lectures (i.e., PowerPoint and audio files play simultaneously) so that the presentation slides advance at predetermined points in the audio file (Griffin, Mitchell, & Thompson, 2009). With unlimited access to the lecture, and access to an index of the words on the slides, students can listen multiple times, take additional notes, and focus on difficult concepts. A wide array of news and other educational content (e.g., iTunes University) is also easily accessible via podcasts.

Duke University pioneered the use of podcasts in higher education and found that students enjoyed using the technology and believed that it enhanced the learning environment (Belanger, 2005). However, many students and faculty expressed some concerns, including the impact of podcasting on attendance and class participation. Recent research has suggested that students' attendance is not affected by the availability of lecture podcasts (Copley, 2007; see Hew, 2009, for a review). Other research has suggested that students enjoy using educational podcasts and report that they are beneficial tools for learning (Evans, 2008; Fernandez, Simo, & Sallan, 2009; McCombs & Liu, 2007; Parson, Reddy, Wood, & Senior, 2009). Interestingly, Griffin et al. (2009) found that students prefer a traditional lecture, but they agreed that it would be beneficial to have podcasts supplement traditional lectures.

Can podcasts improve students' learning? McKinney, Dyck, and Luber (2009) used a nonequivalent group, posttest-only, quasi-experimental design to measure the effectiveness of audio lectures on undergraduate students' learning. All students received a copy of PowerPoint slides, but those in a podcast condition also got a 25-minute podcast of the lecture. Students in the podcast condition scored significantly higher on a related exam. However, only students who took notes on the PowerPoint slides while listening to the podcast performed higher on the exam. The students who did not take notes in the podcast condition scored nearly the same as the in-class lecture students who took notes. McKinney et al. surmised that the students in the podcast condition who took notes were able to take more complete notes because they could control the pace of the lecture (e.g., press pause at any time). In another study, Griffin et al. (2009) found that students with access to a synchronous lecture (i.e., PowerPoint and audio podcast in synchrony) scored significantly higher on multiple-choice exams than students with access to separate media files (i.e., one audio podcast and one PowerPoint file). The researchers posited that providing students with separate files may cause cognitive overload because it is more demanding for the students to manually synchronize audio and visual files on their own (Mayer & Moreno, 2003).

Not all studies support the positive impact of podcasting on learning. Daniel and Woody (2010) found that the students who listened to a podcast scored significantly lower on a related quiz than the students who read the material covered in the podcast. Daniel and Woody suggested that podcasting may not be effective for learning primary material, but the technology may be useful for providing supplemental material (Fernandez et al., 2009).

Additional research is needed to explore the effects of podcasting on teaching and learning. First, a key area of interest is which types of courses would benefit from podcasts. Second, future research should focus on the pedagogical benefits of student-created educational podcasts, which may allow for greater student engagement and a deeper understanding of the course content (e.g., Lee, McLoughlin, & Chan, 2008). Third, additional research should examine how students use podcasts to learn course content (McKinney et al., 2009). For instance, if students take notes while listening to podcasts, are their notes more complete or accurate than those of students who attend actual, real-time lectures? Fourth, if instructors provide podcasts of lectures, there may be an effect on attendance. As mentioned previously, it is important to conduct true experiments and measure the impact of podcast availability on actual class attendance. Finally, it is necessary to examine how the characteristics of the learner (e.g., motivation, personality) are related to podcasting. For example, there is evidence that podcasting increases students' motivation, which may then lead to better learning (Fernandez et al., 2009).

Many studies have shown that quizzing students on reading assignments increases learning (e.g., Connor-Greene, 2000) and that administering online quizzes outside of class can be an effective alternative to traditional in-class quizzing. Johnson and Kiviniemi (2009) found that the completion of required online quizzes predicted higher exam and final course grades. Moreover, online quizzes save class time and require less time for grading (Daniel & Broida, 2004). In addition, recent research has suggested that online testing reduces text anxiety in those students with high test anxiety (Stowell & Bennett, 2010).

Although many instructors rely on online quizzing, researchers have cautioned that unproctored online quizzes are not invariably beneficial in increasing student learning (Brothen & Wambach, 2001; Daniel & Broida, 2004). For instance, students who adopt a "quiz-to-learn" strategy do not benefit from online quizzing. Instead of mastering course content, students who use this strategy try to maximize quiz scores by looking up answers in the book or working with a classmate. There are several ways to discourage students from using this ineffective strategy. First, evidence has suggested that setting time limits on quizzes improves mastery of content (Brothen & Wambach, 2004). By restricting the amount of time allowed for each quiz, students are more likely to rely on an effective strategy for actually learning the course material. Second, instructors should use a large pool of questions so that each student receives a random subset of questions, discouraging working on a quiz with classmates and encouraging students to learn the content better (Daniel & Broida, 2004; Johnson & Kiviniemi, 2009). Third, providing students with feedback after each question, such as where the content is located in the textbook, increases the likelihood that they will master the material (Daniel & Broida, 2004; Johnson & Kiviniemi, 2009). Finally, if academic dishonesty is a concern, adopting an honor code will likely reduce cheating on online tests (Gurung, Wilhelm, & Filtz, in press; Schwartz, Tatum, & Wells, 2012).

Further research is necessary to explore the efficacy of online testing. First, because past research has focused on multiple-choice items (Brothen & Wambach, 2001, 2004; Daniel & Broida, 2004; Johnson & Kiviniemi, 2009), future studies should examine the effect of using essay and short-answer items. Moreover, additional research is needed to determine the characteristics of the students who most benefit from online testing (Stowell & Bennett, 2010). Finally, systematically exploring several key variables (e.g., question difficulty, time limit, course content) should provide a better understanding of how online testing affects learning outcomes (Johnson & Kiviniemi, 2009). Best practice tips for using online testing are summarized in Brothen, Daniel, and Finley (2004).

## WEB 2.0: BLOGS, WIKIS, AND MORE

The term *Web 2.0* commonly refers to the social, collaborative, and interactive applications on the World Wide Web. Web 2.0 tools, such as blogs, wikis, instant messaging, and social-networking technologies allow students and instructors to collaborate in new ways.

A *blog* is a type of technology that allows an individual to post and publish a sequence of entries on a website. As an educational tool, blogs allow students and faculty to share information, publish ideas, collaborate on group projects, and review other people's work.

Recently, instructors have started to explore the use of blogs to enhance teaching and learning (Churchill, 2009; Dyrud, Worley, & Flatley, 2005; Hsu, 2008; Martindale & Wiley, 2005; Richardson, 2006). For instance, Dyrud et al. (2005) used blogs to facilitate group work. Students used the blog to share ideas, review their peers' work, and post work schedules to delineate tasks. Students read and wrote more than past students who did not use blogging. In addition, students mentioned that using blogs enhanced their motivation. In a related study, students reported that blogging enhanced their learning because they learned from reading other people's blogs and receiving comments on their own work from others (Churchill, 2009). Overall, the scant research has suggested that blogging can be an effective educational tool, but additional empirical work testing the impact on learning is essential.

*Wikis* are interlinked web pages developed by two or more people (e.g., Wikipedia). For instance, faculty can post teaching ideas on the Society for the Teaching of Psychology wiki (http://topix.teachpsych.org), which increases the sharing of information. Within minutes, and free of charge, anyone with Internet access can create a wiki (e.g., http://www.pbworks.com).

Using wikis has several potential benefits. A wiki can help students collaborate on group writing projects and improve their writing skills. In one study, students reported concentrating more on writing assignments because they knew that other people were reading their contributions (Wheeler & Wheeler, 2009). Furthermore, wikis may promote a sense of community, allowing students and faculty to interact outside of the traditional classroom asynchronously, facilitating the assignment of group projects. Faculty can also track the input of each individual student on a group assignment, allowing individual grading of students' contributions to the final joint product.

There are potential drawbacks of using wikis. First, because many students are not familiar with the concept of wikis, they may be uncertain of the requirements at the beginning of a wiki assignment (Wheeler, Yeomans, & Wheeler, 2008). Second, if a large number of students are involved in creating a wiki, it becomes increasingly difficult for an instructor to track individual changes to a document (Cronin, 2009). Finally, research has suggested that some students are reluctant to edit their classmates' work, and some become upset when their work is edited by their peers (Cronin, 2009; Wang & Beasley, 2008; Wheeler et al., 2008). To overcome these issues, faculty should devote class time to prepare students for wiki projects (Cronin, 2009). Moreover, providing a low-stakes practice exercise may increase students' confidence and provide an opportunity for students to ask questions (Cronin, 2009; Wheeler et al., 2008). Finally, instead of waiting until the end of a project to assign final grades, constructive feedback should be provided periodically to reinforce students' contributions and encourage greater collaboration (Cronin, 2009).

*Instant messaging* involves two individuals interacting online in a real-time synchronous discussion. Although few instructors have adopted the technology for educational purposes, instant messaging may be a useful pedagogical tool for several reasons (Hsu, 2008). For one, instructors can use instant messaging to hold virtual office hours, thereby increasing their ability to interact with students, at least virtually, and potentially increasing student engagement (Hickerson & Giglio, 2009). Second, students can use instant messaging to collaborate on assignments and projects outside of classroom. Finally, real-time class discussions can take place via instant messaging. For instance, Kinzie, Whitaker, and Hofer (2005) used instant messaging during lectures to encourage all students to participate in class discussions. Although students reported that they were distracted by the task, instant messaging during class may be beneficial because it is an efficient use of time (e.g., students do not have to leave their seats to form discussion groups), it is less distracting because there is less noise, and students can save a record of their discussion for future use.

A number of emerging technologies have surfaced that support social connectedness and provide opportunities for undergraduate education (e.g., Facebook, Myspace, Twitter, Second Life). Faculty can create Facebook pages for their courses to facilitate communication among students in their classes and for students to work together on group projects (Rosales, 2009). Twittering could foster interaction outside of the classroom by allowing students and faculty to communicate ideas, course announcements, and assignment tips (Dunlap & Lowenthal, 2009; Hodges, 2010). Many institutions are experimenting with virtual worlds to enhance teaching and learning (Stevens, Kruck, Hawkins, & Baker, 2010). Second Life, for example, allows students and faculty to meet in an entirely virtual world that replaces the traditional classroom (Baker, Wentz, & Woods, 2009; Walker, 2009; Warburton, 2009).

To date, very little research has focused on the effects of blogs, wikis, instant messaging, and social networking on learning outcomes. Therefore, future research is necessary to examine best practices and the effects of Web 2.0 tools on teaching and learning. Still, it is clear that they are powerful tools for encouraging interaction and collaboration.

# CONCLUSION

Exhibits 3.1 and 3.2 summarize the empirically based best practices for the use of technology and future directions for SoTL on this topic. It is important to note, however, that the domain of technology, perhaps more so than many other areas related to teaching and learning, is evolving in extraordinarily rapid ways. New technologies are constantly being developed, students' familiarity and comfort levels with technology are changing, and the number of studies investigating the efficacy of particular technologies is increasing at a rapid pace. In addition, even when a promising technology is supported by research, the effect on teaching and learning may weaken as the technology becomes more commonplace. Therefore, examination of SoTL findings, including effect sizes, should influence instructors who are selecting and implementing new technologies. We hope that this chapter encourages others to test some of the remaining empirical questions.

For instructors who wish to implement technology in their classes, there are several challenges. Identifying new technologies is just the first step. Instructors must choose technologies that interface with their college's course management system. Preparation time is always substantial, far longer than one anticipates. Furthermore, because students have widely varying abilities and backgrounds using technology, implementation in a class may take up considerable class time.

Still, we believe that the time and effort to implement technology are worthwhile. The nature of students is changing. Whether they are dubbed "net generation students" or given some other moniker, students are increasingly open to the use of technologies (Tapscott, 2008). The familiarity with computers and other technologies that students (some of whom have been using technology since infancy) bring to the classroom requires instructors to at least consider introducing technology into their classroom. In fact, we would argue it is not whether one should introduce technology to the classroom, but which technology to introduce.

Ultimately, though, it is important for both instructors and students to understand that good teaching is good teaching (Christopherson, 2011; Hardin, 2007; Zapf & Garcia, 2011). Technology represents neither a panacea nor an apocalypse for the teaching enterprise. The same principles that relate to good teaching in any domain (e.g., the importance of challenging students, presenting clear goals, holding high expectations, involving and engaging students) underlie teaching whether or not an instructor uses any technology. In the end, the quality of teaching is more important than the implementation of new technology. Consequently, it is up to instructors to use technology as a tool to facilitate good teaching practices.

## EXHIBIT 3.1
## Evidence-Based Recommendations

For presentation software
- Incorporate animation and relevant videos to enhance student learning (Mayer & Moreno, 2003).
- Provide cues (e.g., arrows, headings) for essential content (Mayer & Moreno, 2003).
- Divide the presentation into small segments, allowing the audience time to digest each segment (Mayer & Moreno, 2003).
- Eliminate extraneous material (e.g., background music, images; Bartsch & Cobern, 2003; Mayer & Moreno, 2003).
- Spatially align text with corresponding images to reduce visual scanning (Mayer & Moreno, 2003).
- If providing access to presentation slides, provide partial notes rather than full notes (Barnett, 2003; Cornelius & Owen-DeSchryver, 2008).

For audience response systems
- To minimize anxiety and wasted time, train students to use clickers (Caldwell, 2007).
- Create a plan for dealing with technological difficulties and for students who forget or do not have access to their clickers (Caldwell, 2007).
- Design high-quality clicker activities and questions to maximize student learning (Caldwell, 2007; Kay & LeSage, 2009).
- Use clickers every class meeting to increase student attendance, participation, and engagement (Burnstein & Lederman, 2001; Hunsinger, Poirier, & Feldman, 2008; Poirier & Feldman, 2007; Trees & Jackson, 2007).
- Use clickers to collect feedback from students during a lecture (Abrahamson, 2006; Hake, 1998).
- Provide time in class to discuss results of clicker activities (Kay & LeSage, 2009).
- Because responses are anonymous, use clickers when asking controversial questions (Stowell & Nelson, 2007; Stowell, Oldham, & Bennett, 2010).

For podcasting
- Use podcasts to complement traditional teaching methods (Fernandez, Simo, & Sallan, 2009).
- Do not rely on podcasting to deliver primary course content (Daniel & Woody, 2010).
- If a podcast accompanies a presentation, synchronize the audio and PowerPoint files (Griffin, Mitchell, & Thompson, 2009).
- Encourage students to take notes while they listen to podcasts (McKinney, Dyck, & Luber, 2009).

For online testing
- Implement time limits to discourage the "quiz-to-learn" strategy (Brothen & Wambach, 2004).
- Use a large pool of questions to reduce cheating (Daniel & Broida, 2004; Johnson & Kiviniemi, 2009).
- Provide feedback after each question (Daniel & Broida, 2004; Johnson & Kiviniemi, 2009).
- Require students to complete quizzes before content is covered in class (Johnson & Kiviniemi, 2009).
- Administer online tests for students with high levels of test anxiety (Stowell & Bennett, 2010).

## EXHIBIT 3.2
## Questions for Future Research

For presentation software
- What are the effects of different software (e.g., Apple Keynote)?
- How are student behaviors, including note taking and studying, influenced by having access to presentations before and after class?
- What are the effects of the type of content (e.g., text, images) that instructors put on their slides, as well as any supplemental information they provide to their students?

For audience response systems
- What is the relationship between student characteristics (e.g., students' personality traits) and the efficacy of using clickers?
- What types of questions are most effective for specific learning environments?

For podcasting
- Which types of courses would most benefit from podcasts?
- How do students use podcasts to learn course content?
- What are the pedagogical benefits of student-created educational podcasts?
- How does podcast availability affect actual class attendance?
- How do the characteristics of the learner (e.g., motivation) relate to podcasting?

For online testing
- What are the effects of using essay and short-answer items?
- What are the characteristics of the students who most benefit from online testing?

For Web 2.0 tools
- What are the best uses of these technologies?

## REFERENCES

Abrahamson, L. (2006). A brief history of networked classrooms: Effects, cases, pedagogy, and implications. In D. A. Banks (Ed.), *Audience response systems in higher education* (pp. 1–25). Hershey, PA: Information Science Publishing. doi:10.4018/978-1-59140-947-2.ch001

Apperson, J. M., Laws, E. L., & Scepansky, J. A. (2006). The impact of presentation graphics on students' experience in the classroom. *Computers & Education, 47,* 116–126. doi:10. 1016/j.compedu.2004.09.003

Axtell, K., Maddux, C., & Aberasturi, S. (2008). The effect of presentation software on classroom verbal interaction and on student retention of higher education lecture content. *International Journal of Technology in Teaching and Learning, 4,* 21–33. Retrieved from http://www.sicet.org/journals/ijttl/ijttl.html

Babb, K. A., & Ross, C. (2009). The timing of online lecture slide availability and its effect on attendance, participation, and exam performance. *Computers & Education, 52,* 868–881. doi:10.1016/j.compedu.2008.12.009

Baker, S. C., Wentz, R. K., & Woods, M. M. (2009). Using virtual worlds in education: Second Life as an educational tool. *Teaching of Psychology, 36,* 59–64. doi:10.1080/00986280802529079

Barnett, J. E. (2003). Do instructor-provided online notes facilitate student learning? *The Journal of Interactive Online Learning, 2*(2), 1–7. Retrieved from http://www.ncolr.org/

Bartsch, R. A., & Cobern, K. M. (2003). Effectiveness of PowerPoint presentations in lectures. *Computers & Education, 41,* 77–86. doi:10.1016/S0360-1315(03)00027-7

Beatty, I. D. (2004). Transforming student learning with classroom communication systems. *EDUCAUSE Research Bulletin, 2004*(3), 1–13. Retrieved from http://srri.umass.edu/publications/Beatty-2004tsl

Belanger, Y. (2005, June). *Duke University iPod first year experience final evaluation report.* Retrieved from http://cit.duke.edu/pdf/reports/ipod_initiative_04_05.pdf

Bowman, L. L. (2009). Does posting PowerPoint presentations on WebCT affect class performance or attendance? *Journal of Instructional Psychology, 36,* 104–107.

Brothen, T., Daniel, D. B., & Finley, D. L. (2004, December). *Best principles in the use of online quizzing.* Paper prepared for the Society for the Teaching of Psychology Pedagogical Innovations Task Force. Retrieved from http://www.apadiv2.org/resources/pedagogy/onlinetesting.pdf

Brothen, T., & Wambach, C. (2001). Effective student use of computerized quizzes. *Teaching of Psychology, 28,* 292–294. doi:10.1207/S15328023TOP2804_10

Brothen, T., & Wambach, C. (2004). The value of time limits on internet quizzes. *Teaching of Psychology, 31,* 62–64. doi:10.1207/s15328023top3101_12

Burnstein, R. A., & Lederman, L. M. (2001). Using wireless keypads in lecture classes. *The Physics Teacher, 39,* 6–11. doi:10.1119/1.1343420

Caldwell, J. E. (2007). Clickers in the large classroom: Current research and best-practice tips. *Life Sciences Education, 6,* 9–20. doi:10.1187/cbe.06-12-0205

Christopherson, K. M. (2011). Hardware or wetware: What are the possible interactions of pedagogy and technology in the classroom? *Teaching of Psychology, 38,* 288–292. doi:10.1177/0098628311421332

Churchill, D. (2009). Educational applications of Web 2.0: Using blogs to support teaching and learning. *British Journal of Educational Technology, 40,* 179–183. doi:10.1111/j.1467-8535.2008.00865.x

Connor-Greene, P. A. (2000). Assessing and promoting student learning: Blurring the line between teaching and testing. *Teaching of Psychology, 27,* 84–88. doi:10.1207/S15328023TOP2702_01

Copley, J. (2007). Audio and video podcasts of lectures for campus-based students: Production and evaluation of student use. *Innovations in Education and Teaching International, 44,* 387–399. doi:10.1080/14703290701602805

Cornelius, T. L., & Owen-DeSchryver, J. (2008). Differential effects of full and partial notes on learning outcomes and attendance. *Teaching of Psychology, 35*, 6–12. doi:10.1080/00986280701818466

Cronin, J. J. (2009). Upgrading to Web 2.0: An experiential project to build a marketing wiki. *Journal of Marketing Education, 31*, 66–75. doi:10.1177/0273475308329250

Crouch, C. H., & Mazur, E. (2001). Peer instruction: Ten years of experience and results. *American Journal of Physics, 69*, 970–977. doi:10.1119/1.1374249

Daniel, D. B., & Broida, J. (2004). Using web-based quizzing to improve exam performance: Lessons learned. *Teaching of Psychology, 31*, 207–208. doi:10.1207/s15328023top3103_6

Daniel, D. B., & Woody, W. D. (2010). They hear, but do not listen: Retention for podcasted material in a classroom context. *Teaching of Psychology, 37*, 199–203. doi:10.1080/00986283.2010.488542

DeBord, K. A., Aruguete, M. S., & Muhlig, J. (2004). Are computer-assisted teaching methods effective? *Teaching of Psychology, 31*, 65–68. doi:10.1207/s15328023 top3101_13

d'Inverno, R., Davis, H., & White, S. (2003). Using a personal response system for promoting student interaction. *Teaching Mathematics and Its Applications, 22*, 163–169. doi:10.1093/teamat/22.4.163

Draper, S. W., & Brown, M. I. (2004). Increasing interactivity in lectures using an electric voting system. *Journal of Computer Assisted Learning, 20*, 81–94. doi:10.1111/j.1365-2729.2004.00074.x

Dunlap, J. C., & Lowenthal, P. R. (2009). Horton hears a tweet. *EDUCAUSE Quarterly, 32*(4). Retrieved from http://www.educause.edu/eq

Dyrud, M. A., Worley, R. B., & Flatley, M. E. (2005). Blogging for enhanced teaching and learning. *Business Communication Quarterly, 68*, 77–80. Retrieved from http://bcq.sagepub.com/ doi:10.1177/108056990506800111

Evans, C. (2008). The effectiveness of m-learning in the form of podcast revision lectures in higher education. *Computers & Education, 50*, 491–498. doi:10.1016/jcompedu.2007.09.016

Fernandez, V., Simo, P., & Sallan, J. (2009). Podcasting: A new technological tool to facilitate good practice in higher education. *Computers & Education, 53*, 385–392. doi:10.1016/j.compedu.2009.02.014

Frank, J., Shaw, L., & Wilson, E. (2008-2009). The impact of providing web-based PowerPoint slides as study guides in undergraduate business classes. *Journal of Educational Technology Systems, 37*, 217–229. doi:10.2190/ET.37.2.g

Frey, B. A., & Birnbaum, D. J. (2002). *Learners' perceptions on the value of PowerPoint in lectures.* Pittsburgh, PA: University of Pittsburgh. (ERIC Document Reproduction Services No. ED467192)

Griffin, D. K., Mitchell, D., & Thompson, S. J. (2009). Podcasting by synchronising PowerPoint and voice: What are the pedagogical benefits? *Computers & Education, 53*, 532–539. doi:10.1016/j.compedu.2009.03.011

Gurung, R. A. R., Wilhelm, T., & Filtz, T. (in press). Optimizing honor codes for online exam administration. *Ethics & Behavior.*

Hake, R. (1998). Interactive engagement versus traditional methods: A six-thousand student survey of mechanics test data for introductory physics courses. *American Journal of Physics, 66,* 64–74. doi:10.1119/1.18809

Hardin, E. E. (2007). Presentation software in the college classroom: Don't forget the instructor. *Teaching of Psychology, 34,* 53–57. doi:10.1207/s15328023top3401_13

Hew, K. F. (2009). Use of audio podcast in K-12 and higher education: A review of research topics and methodologies. *Educational Technology Research and Development, 57,* 333–357. doi:10.1007/s11423-008-9108-3

Hickerson, C. A., & Giglio, M. (2009). Instant messaging between students and faculty: A tool for increasing student-faculty interaction. *International Journal on E-Learning, 8,* 71–88. Retrieved from http://www.aace.org/pubs/ijel/

Hlynka, D., & Mason, R. (1998). "PowerPoint" in the classroom: What is the point? *Educational Technology, 38,* 45–48.

Hodges, C. B. (2010). If you Twitter, will they come? *EDUCAUSE Quarterly, 33(2).* Retrieved from http://www.educause.edu/eq

Hoekstra, A. (2008). Vibrant student voices: Exploring effects of the use of clickers in large college courses. *Learning, Media & Technology, 33,* 329–341. doi:10.1080/17439880802497081

Hove, M. C., & Corcoran, K. J. (2008a). Educational technologies: Impact on learning and frustration. *Teaching of Psychology, 35,* 121–125. doi:10.1080/00986280802004578

Hove, M. C., & Corcoran, K. J. (2008b). If you post it, will they come? Lecture availability in introductory psychology. *Teaching of Psychology, 35,* 91–95. doi:10.1080/00986280802004560

Hsu, J. (2008). Innovative technologies for education and learning: Education and knowledge-oriented applications of blogs, wikis, podcasts, and more. *International Journal of Web-Based Learning and Teaching Technologies, 3,* 62–81. Retrieved from http://www.igi-pub.com/Bookstore/TitleDetails.aspx?TitleId=1081 doi:10.4018/jwltt.2008070106

Hunsinger, M., Poirier, C. R., & Feldman, R. S. (2008). The roles of personality and class size in student attitudes toward individual response technology. *Computers in Human Behavior, 24,* 2792–2798. doi:10.1016/j.chb.2008.04.003

Johnson, B. C., & Kiviniemi, M. T. (2009). The effect of online chapter quizzes on exam performance in an undergraduate social psychology course. *Teaching of Psychology, 36,* 33–37. doi:10.1080/00986280802528972

Kay, R. H., & LeSage, A. (2009). Examining the benefits and challenges of using audience response systems: A review of the literature. *Computers & Education, 53,* 819–827. doi:10.1016/j.compedu.2009.05.001

Kennedy, G. E., & Cutts, Q. I. (2005). The association between students' use of an electronic voting system and their learning outcomes. *Journal of Computer Assisted Learning, 21,* 260–268. doi:10.1111/j.1365-2729.2005.00133.x

Kinzie, M. B., Whitaker, S. D., & Hofer, M. J. (2005). Instructional uses of instant messaging (IM) during classroom lectures. *Journal of Educational Technology & Society, 8,* 150–160. Retrieved from http://www.ifets.info/others/

Lee, M. J. W., McLoughlin, C., & Chan, A. (2008). Talk the talk: Learner-generated podcasts as catalysts for knowledge creation. *British Journal of Educational Technology, 39,* 501–521. doi:10.1111/j.1467-8535.2007.00746.x

Ludwig, T. E., Daniel, D. B., Froman, R., & Mathie, V. A. (2004, December). *Using multimedia in classroom presentations: Best principles.* Paper prepared for the Society for the Teaching of Psychology Pedagogical Innovations Task Force. Retrieved from http://www.apadiv2.org/resources/pedagogy/classroommultimedia.pdf

Martindale, T., & Wiley, D. A. (2005). Using weblogs in scholarship and teaching. *TechTrends, 59,* 55–61. Retrieved from http://www.aect.org/Intranet/Publications/index.asp#tt

Mayer, R. E., & Moreno, R. (2003). Nine ways to reduce cognitive load in multimedia learning. *Educational Psychologist, 38,* 43–52. doi:10.1207/S15326985EP3801_6

Mayer, R. E., Stull, A., DeLeeuw, K., Almeroth, K., Bimber, B., Chun, D., ... Zhang, H. (2009). Clickers in college classrooms: Fostering learning with questioning methods in large lecture classes. *Contemporary Educational Psychology, 34,* 51–57. doi:10.1016/j.cedpsych.2008.04.002

McCombs, S., & Liu, Y. (2007). The efficacy of podcasting technology in instructional delivery. *International Journal of Technology in Teaching and Learning, 3,* 123–134. Retrieved from http://www.sicet.org/journals/ijttl/ijttl.html

McKinney, D., Dyck, J. L., & Luber, E. S. (2009). iTunes University and the classroom: Can podcasts replace professors? *Computers & Education, 52,* 617–623. doi:10.1016/j.compedu.2008.11.004

Millis, K., Baker, S., Blakemore, J. E. O., Connington, F., Harper, Y. Y., Hung, W., ... Stowell, J. (2010). Teaching and learning in a digital world. In D. F. Halpern (Ed.), *Undergraduate education in psychology: A blueprint for the future of the discipline* (pp. 113–128). Washington, DC: American Psychological Association. doi:10.1037/12063-007

Morling, B., McAuliffe, M., Cohen, L., & DiLorenzo, T. M. (2008). Efficacy of personal response systems ("clickers") in large, introductory psychology classes. *Teaching of Psychology, 35,* 45–50. doi:10.1080/00986280701818516

Noppe, I., Achterberg, J., Duquaine, L., Huebbe, M., & Williams, C. (2007). PowerPoint presentation handouts and college student learning outcomes. *International Journal for the Scholarship of Teaching and Learning, 1(1),* 1–13. Retrieved from http://academics.georgiasouthern.edu/ijsotl/index.htm

Parson, V., Reddy, P., Wood, J., & Senior, C. (2009). Educating an iPod generation: Undergraduate attitudes, experiences and understanding of vodcast and podcast use. *Learning, Media and Technology, 34,* 215–228. doi:10.1080/17439880903141497

Patry, M. (2009). Clickers in large classes: From student perceptions towards an understanding of best practices. *International Journal for the Scholarship of*

*Teaching and Learning, 3*(2), 1–11. Retrieved from http://academics.georgia-southern.edu/ijsotl/

Pemberton, J. R., Borrego, J., Jr., & Cohen, L. M. (2006). Using interactive computer technology to enhance learning. *Teaching of Psychology, 33,* 145–147. doi:10.1207/s15328023top3302

Poirier, C. R., & Feldman, R. S. (2007). Promoting active learning using individual response technology in large introductory psychology classes. *Teaching of Psychology, 34,* 194–196. doi:10.1080/00986280701498665

Richardson, W. (2006). *Blogs, wikis, podcasts, and other powerful web tools for classrooms.* Thousand Oaks, CA: Corwin Press.

Rosales, R. (2009). Eight simple ways to embrace the "Froom." *EDUCAUSE Quarterly, 32*(4). Retrieved from http://www.educause.edu/eq

Schwartz, B. M., Tatum, H. E., & Wells, J. W. (2012). The honor system: Influences on attitudes, behaviors, and pedagogy. In R. E. Landrum & M. A. McCarthy (Eds.), *Teaching ethically: Challenges and opportunities* (pp. 89–98). Washington, DC: American Psychological Association. doi:10.1037/13496-000

Stevens, K. E., Kruck, S. E., Hawkins, J., & Baker, S. C. (2010). Second Life as a tool for engaging students across the curriculum. In P. Zemliansky & D. Wilcox (Eds.), *Design and implementation of educational games: Theoretical and practical perspectives* (pp. 378–392). doi:10.4018/978-1-61520-781-7.ch024

Stowell, J. R., & Bennett, D. (2010). Effects of online testing on student exam performance and test anxiety. *Journal of Educational Computing Research, 42,* 161–171. doi: 10.2190/EC.42.2.b

Stowell, J. R., & Nelson, J. M. (2007). Benefits of electronic audience response systems on student participation, learning, and emotion. *Teaching of Psychology, 34,* 253–258. doi:10.1080/00986280701700391

Stowell, J. R., Oldham, T., & Bennett, D. (2010). Using student response systems ("clickers") to combat conformity and shyness. *Teaching of Psychology, 37,* 135–140. doi: 10.1080/00986281003626631

Susskind, J. E. (2005). PowerPoint's power in the classroom: Enhancing students' self-efficacy and attitudes. *Computers & Education, 45,* 203–215. doi:10.1016/j.compedu.2004.07.005

Susskind, J. E. (2008). Limits of PowerPoint's power: Enhancing students' self-efficacy and attitudes but not their behavior. *Computers & Education, 50,* 1228–1239. doi:10.1016/j.compedu.2006.12.001

Szabo, A., & Hastings, N. (2000). Using IT in the undergraduate classroom: Should we replace the Blackboard with PowerPoint? *Computers & Education, 35,* 175–187. doi:10.1016/S0360-1315(00)00030-0

Tapscott, D. (2008). *Grown up digital.* New York, NY: McGraw-Hill.

Trees, A. R., & Jackson, M. H. (2007). The learning environment in clicker classrooms: Student processes of learning and involvement in large university-level courses using student response systems. *Learning, Media & Technology, 32,* 21–40. doi:10.1080/17439880601141179

Tufte, E. R. (2004). *The cognitive style of PowerPoint.* Cheshire, CT: Graphics.

Walker, V. L. (2009). 3D virtual learning in counselor education: Using Second Life in counselor skill development. *Journal of Virtual Worlds Research, 2,* 3–14. Retrieved from http://jvwresearch.org/

Wang, L., & Beasley, W. (2008). The wiki as a web 2.0 tool in education. *International Journal of Technology in Teaching and Learning, 4,* 78–85. Retrieved from http://www.sicet.org/journals/ijttl/ijttl.html

Warburton, S. (2009). Second Life in higher education: Assessing the potential for and the barriers to deploying virtual worlds in learning and teaching. *British Journal of Educational Technology, 40,* 414–426. doi:10.1111/j.1467-8535.2009.00952.x

Wheeler, S., & Wheeler, D. (2009). Using wikis to promote quality learning in teacher training. *Learning, Media and Technology, 34,* 1–10. doi:10.1080/17439880902759851

Wheeler, S., Yeomans, P., & Wheeler, D. (2008). The good, the bad and the wiki: Evaluating student-generated content for collaborative learning. *British Journal of Educational Technology, 39,* 987–995. doi:10.1111/j.1467-8535.2007.00799.x

Zapf, J. A., & Garcia, A. J. (2011). The influence of tech-savvyness and clicker use on student learning. *International Journal for the Scholarship of Teaching and Learning, 5*(1), 1–11. Retrieved from http://academics.georgiasouthern.edu/ijsotl/index.htm

# 4

# ONLINE TEACHING

CHANDRA M. MEHROTRA AND LAWRENCE McGAHEY

Online education is a form of distance education delivered across the Internet. In online courses, at least 80% of the instructional content is delivered through the web, typically without face-to-face meetings (Allen & Seaman, 2007). Hybrid instructional models, those combining traditional in-seat meetings with online sessions, are also becoming increasingly common. For a historical perspective regarding the growth of distance education programs in the United States and an overview of important factors in initiating an online program, see Mehrotra, Hollister, and McGahey (2001).

Online education can be differentiated as *synchronous* delivery (instructor and student are online at the same time) or *asynchronous* delivery (instructor and student need not be in direct contact through the Internet at the same time). The asynchronous delivery of instruction attracts many students because it affords greater learner control in balancing education, work, and family life (Hrastinski, 2008), although online courses commonly blend synchronous and asynchronous elements. This chapter concentrates on the role of the effective instructor in asynchronously delivered online courses. We review the essentials of online teaching, including the characteristics of online students, the factors that should be considered in designing an online course, the instructional methods most effective in fostering student learning, and methods available to assess learning outcomes.

# REASONS TO OFFER AND ENROLL IN ONLINE COURSES

Online offerings afford bricks-and-mortar institutions an opportunity to fulfill their mission objectives through outreach to a larger population of students without the expense of constructing additional facilities. The online enterprise can also be a profitable addition supporting the traditional on-campus delivery model. Findings from the literature can begin to inform us of the pedagogical choices to consider when teaching online.

The ability to use and deliver multiple forms of instructional materials directly to the student, augmented by the student's opportunity to revisit course content at will, is especially attractive as it holds the promise of greater student engagement in active learning than is typical in the standard class-room (Rudestam, 2004). A 12-year meta-analysis of research by the U.S. Department of Education (2009) indicated that students who took all or part of a course online performed better on objective measures of learning (e.g., standardized tests, assignments, midterm/final exams), on average, than those taking the same course through traditional face-to-face instruction. Hybrid classes were the most effective in enhancing student learning. The conclusions are limited in that the studies analyzed did not use the same curriculum materials (e.g., textbooks), aspects of pedagogy (e.g., lectures, discussion), or learning time in the treatment and control conditions. Thus, the observed advantage for online learning and blended learning conditions that emerged may not be rooted in delivery mode use per se but rather may reflect differences in one or more of these factors among the studies included in the meta-analysis.

Though there are many reasons why students choose to pursue education through online learning, Hannay and Newvine (2006) found that scheduling flexibility, travel time, and distance to campus were the most common factors. The typical undergraduate course schedule for face-to-face instruction does not provide the flexibility needed by students with family responsibilities and/or who are employed. However, personal choice also may prompt students to select online courses in preference to traditional campus offerings. Wang and Newlin (2000) reported that about 80% of distance students also enroll in conventional campus courses.

# CHARACTERISTICS OF ONLINE STUDENTS

A number of characteristics distinguish online learners from their campus counterparts. Compared with traditional on-campus students, online students tend to be older, have accumulated more credits, and have higher cumulative grade-point averages (Diaz, 2002). Students in online (vs. comparable traditional) sections of a course in psychological statistics were more likely to collaborate with different students throughout the semester and spend more hours studying than those in the conventional campus section (Wang & Newlin, 2000). Online students also exhibit higher course dropout rates than are seen on campus, with the decision to drop an online course perhaps reflecting an informed, mature decision by the student that he or she is unable to invest sufficient time and attention to make the experience worthwhile (Diaz, 2002).

Research concerning online courses at the community college level has provided further insights about successful online students (Wojciechowski & Palmer, 2005). Liu, Gomez, and Yen (2009) found that both the retention of students and their success were found to correlate with social presence (Tu, 2002). Students with a positive perception of social presence—those viewing the online environment as a social context in which conversation was informal, conveyed emotion, and was interactive and in which privacy concerns were addressed—were more likely to maintain a high degree of collaboration and interaction online, both of which are essential to the formation and effective continuance of learning communities. Liu et al. recommended early identification of and intervention on behalf of students at risk for dropout through assessment tools, such as Tu's (2002) Social Presence and Privacy Questionnaire.

Online learning by its nature is dependent on and mediated by technology that can enhance or impede learning. Given the reliance on instructional technology in the online environment, it is not surprising that successful online students seek assistance with technical problems as they arise. A preliminary study of experienced teachers in a graduate program demonstrated that even those who rate themselves as highly proficient computer-technology users may still have deficiencies that impede their access to course materials and other students. Thus, students can benefit from early advising about specific types of technology with which they are less familiar (Blocher, de Montes, Willis, & Tucker, 2002) and from accessible technical support.

Successful online students also tend to be independent and to possess an internal locus of control (Wang & Newlin, 2000). Effective online students establish how much interaction is required with the instructor and other students, when assignments are due, and when they need to actively seek clarification of instructions in advance of deadlines. Consistent with the findings of Blocher et al. (2002), these results also indicate that successful online students know how to find out whom to contact for technical problems related to hardware or software and how to execute any instructions correctly. In short, successful online students demonstrate self-regulation and can monitor their own motivation and resources (Bell & Akroyd, 2006; Blocher et al., 2002). More experienced students or workers are likely to have mastered meeting the expectations of supervisors and thus may have an advantage over younger, inexperienced online students.

## FOSTERING SELF-REGULATION AMONG ONLINE STUDENTS

Evidence regarding the importance of self-regulation in online courses has suggested that students, especially those who are new to online instruction, should be afforded information, assessment, and training to develop appropriate self-regulatory habits and mind-set. Effective instructors use a variety of approaches to foster the development of self-regulation among learners. Findings from numerous studies (Bixler, 2008; Chang, 2007; Chung, Chung, & Severance, 1999; Cook, Dupras, Thompson, & Pankratz, 2005; Crippen & Earl, 2007; Saito & Miwa, 2007) have indicated that a tool or feature prompting students to monitor their learning improves online learning outcomes (e.g., grades). Examples of such tools include questions at the end of each unit that ask students to outline the train of thought they used in arriving at an answer; forms on which students record study time, note their learning process, predict their test scores, and create a self-evaluation; and instructional features such as glossaries, self-tests, multimedia materials, and supplementary information (Svinicki & McKeachie, 2009). These prompts and features help students learn how to explain concepts to themselves, stay on task, note gaps in their comprehension, plan ahead, self-correct errors, and apportion time and effort. Engagement in metacognitive monitoring— tracking how well they have or have not acquired skills and knowledge— can be as important as the actual levels of skills and knowledge. In sum, research has suggested that engaging students in self-reflection, self-regulation, and self-monitoring helps them achieve the intended learning outcomes (U.S. Department of Education, 2009). Effective online instructors provide content knowledge and also teach their students how to become strategic, self-regulated learners in their field of study.

## WHAT FACTORS SHOULD BE CONSIDERED IN DESIGNING AN ONLINE COURSE?

Four key factors need to be considered in developing and/or selecting an online course: the goals of the course, the prior knowledge of the learners, the course environment, and the instructional architecture.

### Goals

The goals or intended outcomes of a course should influence the choice of instructional methods and media elements used (Wiggins & McTighe, 2005). When the goal is to provide students new information, instruction using a multimedia presentation—words (printed text or spoken text) combined with graphics (static drawings or animations, video)—is more effective than using words alone (Clark & Mayer, 2008). In general, students provided with a multimedia lesson perform better on a subsequent transfer test than their counterparts instructed by words alone (Mayer, 1989; Mayer & Anderson, 1991; Moreno & Mayer, 1999, 2002). Of note, static illustrations are not a poorer choice than animations (Clark & Mayer, 2008), although some content is particularly better suited to animation or video (ChanLin, 1998). Clark and Mayer (2008) further recommended that instructors insert words in spoken form rather than printed form whenever the graphic (animation or static frames) is the focus of words and both are presented simultaneously. This recommendation is based on the modality principle, supported by a number of experimental studies (see, e.g., Craig, Gholson, & Driscoll, 2002; Mayer, Dow, & Mayer, 2003; Moreno & Mayer, 1999). A meta-analysis by Ginns (2005) presented strong evidence for the modality effect and also indicated that the positive effect of auditory delivery is stronger for more complex material. Additional research is needed to determine (a) what types of visuals are more effective for different learners and instructional objectives and (b) what role is played by color graphics in fostering student learning.

### Learners' Prior Knowledge

Instructional materials and methods should be appropriate to the individual differences among students. Although individual characteristics on variables such as abilities, aptitudes, and learning styles have received much attention, research has clearly indicated that students' prior knowledge of the course content exerts the most influence on their learning (Ollerenshaw, Aidman, & Kidd, 1997). In a course for a less advanced group of learners, it would be beneficial to supplement text-based instruction with coordinated graphics; however, in a course for more advanced learners, text alone should be sufficient.

### Course Environment

The online environment encompasses the technical constraints, institutional cultural factors, and resource limitations that affect online learning and teaching. Technical constraints include issues pertaining to the type of software used to manage course content (e.g., open source), whether students and instructors must install specific software on their computer, and the functional modules the software provides (e.g., chat room). Students also need to know in advance of any hardware (e.g., audiovisual peripherals) required to fully access the teaching tools embedded in content delivery software. Faculty planning to teach online should consider whether this delivery mode is valued comparably to conventional on-campus teaching in workload and promotion-tenure decisions. Is the institution collectively committed to the online model—that is, is there sufficient campus experience and acceptance of teaching online that the faculty member will not be distracted from teaching by having to spend time defending this mode of delivery? Instructors must make choices and adaptations for teaching that reflect the realities of the local environmental support for their online efforts. They need to be wary of using new technology simply because of its "wow" factor; that is, does the technology truly support the educational goals of the course, or is it merely the newest fad?

## Course Architecture

Over time, three views of learning have evolved: information acquisition, response strengthening, and knowledge construction (Clark & Mayer, 2008). A course designed with an information acquisition view of learning will use a receptive architecture in which the instructor will be the dispenser of information and the learner will be a passive recipient of the information with little or no interaction with the content, other learners, or the instructor. Using a response-strengthening outlook on learning, lessons follow a sequence of "explanation–example–questions–feedback" commonly designed for helping learners develop skills such as designing software or performing statistical computations. The directive architecture provides highly structured practice opportunities aimed at guiding learning in a step-by-step manner. Directive courses or units have a medium-range of interactivity; learners interact with the instructional material, but not necessarily with other learners. The instructor's role lies mainly in designing instructional units, monitoring students' progress, and providing them feedback on an ongoing basis. The knowledge construction view of learning uses guided discovery. An excellent example of this architecture is provided by simulation and games. In contrast to the information acquisition view of learning, the knowledge construction framework considers students to be active sense makers: Learners engage in active cognitive processing during learning. Thus, learners are seen as attending to relevant information, mentally organizing it into a coherent structure and integrating it with what they already know.

## PRACTICAL MATTERS

Teaching online requires additional consideration of some practical matters. For valuable practical guides, see Boettcher and Conrad, 2010, and Rudestam and Schoenholtz-Read, 2002. These references provide valuable guidance that is based on empirical research. In addition, those new to online teaching might consider developing a mentor relationship with a colleague who has taught online for several terms.

## The Syllabus

Online syllabi need not be bound by the limitations of the printed page because the medium is different. Thus, embedded links to audio, video, and other sites can enliven the syllabus (Miller, 2009). Links leading to other pages containing more detailed information can make the syllabus appear less monolithic as well (Hayes, 2007; Mostyn, 2009). Instructors should bear in mind that font size, type, and color can communicate tone as well as convey unintended meanings (Betts, 2009). Once the document is in service online, recurring questions about the same item suggest that some rewording or a "frequently asked questions" page is needed.

## Instructional Methods

In this section, we briefly describe four key instructional methods and discuss how each exploits the potential of information technology to foster student learning in creative ways.

### Practice With Automatic Tailored Feedback

Effective online instruction provides learners with opportunities for deliberate practice that focuses on specific gaps in knowledge or skills and offers explanatory corrective feedback (Ericsson, 2006). For example, after the learner responds to a given question, he or she is provided feedback that not only indicates whether the answer is correct or incorrect but also provides a succinct explanation (Debowski, Wood, & Bandura, 2001).

### Integration of Collaboration With Self-Study

According to Chickering and Gamson (1991), good learning, like good work, is collaborative and social rather than competitive and isolated, and working with others increases involvement in learning. Effective online courses engage students in discussions, collaborative projects, and group assignments (Althaus, 1997; Uribe, Klein, & Sullivan, 2003). It is likely that working together allows the participants to compare alternative interpretations and situations, correct each other's misconceptions, and form more holistic pictures of problems.

In general, the use of asynchronous discussion is viewed positively by online students (Ocker & Yaverbaum, 2001; Shaw & Pieter, 2000) and may differ substantially from face-to-face classes (Smith, Ferguson, & Caris,

2002). Meyer (2003) noted that there are advantages to holding discussion in all forms of instructional delivery but reported that students spend more time in online discussion and exhibit higher order thinking through comments that explore the implications of the research they have examined and/or integrate key ideas posted by fellow learners. Shaw and Pieter (2000) observed that students who contributed more frequently to the group online discussion scored significantly better on the final exam. However, research about the impact of ongoing instructor feedback and communication on specific student learning outcomes is rather limited at the present time.

*Dynamic Adjustments of Instruction Based on Learning*

Available software can permit adjustments to the instructional path on the basis of learners' responses to questions embedded in the instructional unit. Thus, if a student makes an error on a question of intermediate complexity, the computer program can offer either an easier problem or another version of the same problem accompanied by increased instructional guidance. Such tailoring of instruction that is based on the learner's progress is called *adaptive instruction,* a feature of online courses that is particularly beneficial when there are substantial individual differences among students regarding prior knowledge related to the content.

Although the number of studies focusing on adaptive instruction is rather limited, studies conducted to date have demonstrated positive effects for the technique. Grant and Courtoreille (2007) investigated the use of postunit quizzes presented either as (a) fixed items that provided feedback only about whether the student's response was correct or (b) postunit quizzes that provided students the opportunity for additional practice on the type of items that they had answered incorrectly. The response-sensitive version of the tutorial was found to be more effective, resulting in greater improvement in test scores between pre- and posttests. This improvement in student learning demonstrates the effectiveness of individualized instruction in which the learners are not only told whether they answered the question correctly but also offered a short explanation of why a given response is correct or incorrect. After receiving this individualized feedback, they are provided the opportunity to practice on the type of items they answered incorrectly.

*Simulations and Games*

The popularity of entertainment games and simulations has led to their inclusion in online instruction as a means to improve learning outcomes. There are two types of simulations: operational and conceptual. *Operational* simulations are designed primarily to teach procedural skills, such as medical procedures and safety-related skills (e.g., aircraft piloting and industrial control operations). In contrast, *conceptual* simulations are designed primarily to help build far-transfer knowledge of a specific domain, as well as associated problem-solving skills. In higher education, conceptual simulations have focused on principles of physics, chemistry, botany, genetics, information technology, and ecology, to name a few. In an online module on information technology for undergraduate psychology students, Castaneda (2008) compared two simulation conditions (self-guided vs. not). Knowledge gains from pre- and posttests were greater for students with either type of simulation, provided they were exposed to it after the expository instruction. In another study, Hilbelink (2007) found that students using three-dimensional images had a small, but significant, advantage in identifying anatomical parts and spatial relationships over students using two-dimensional images.

Games, like simulations, also have a diverse array of formats and features. Elements common to all games include (a) a competitive activity with a challenge to achieve a goal, (b) a set of rules and constraints, and (c) a specific context. Outcome research has indicated that feedback is the single most commonly mentioned success factor among research studies on the effectiveness of simulations and games in improving student learning (Issenberg, McGaghie, Petrusa, Gordon, & Scalese, 2005). Feedback may be built into a simulation or game, provided by an instructor, or provided in a video reviewed after the session; the source of the feedback is less important than its presence (Issenberg et al., 2005). Effective feedback includes a brief instructional explanation of why a given response is correct or incorrect (see Moreno, 2004, for an example).

Although the research has indicated that simulation and games are highly useful, it may not be possible for all instructors to design these materials for their online courses. We recommend they seek out these materials as they become available from a variety of resources.

## ASSESSING STUDENTS' LEARNING IN AN ONLINE COURSE

Ongoing evaluation of student learning becomes even more critical in the absence of face-to-face interactions during which instructors can use informal observations to gauge students' responses to instruction and to monitor their progress. In an online course, assessment methods are embedded in the course modules and administered on a continuing basis. These assessment methods can include self-check quizzes, comprehension tests, application exercises, case studies, and simulations, all of which can be administered through course management software. Continued assessment enables the online instructor to provide immediate feedback to learners often throughout the semester, which creates milestones of accomplishment that help the learners grow toward expected outcomes. Such feedback provides knowledge of results, informs learners whether they answered the question correctly, and offers a short explanation of why a given response is correct or not (Brooks, Nolan, & Gallagher, 2003; Daniel & Broida, 2004). Consistent with early research illustrating that distributed practice yields better long-term retention (Ebbinghaus, 1885/1913), quizzes should be distributed throughout the units for maximal effectiveness (Rawson & Kintsch, 2005). Scores from these practice tests may be used as a small contribution toward course grades as well (Mehrotra et al., 2001).

Next we discuss three methods of assessing student learning (i.e., group discussion, term papers, and tests) and what needs to be considered for an online course for each method. Regardless of the methods chosen, it is critical to ensure that the student who registers is the same student who participates in all activities of the course and completes the work and gets the academic credit. Language related to verifying the identify of students in distance-education programs is now included in the Higher Education Opportunity Act (2008). One can consider using an honor code for online courses. This recommendation is based on a series of empirical studies that have demonstrated a positive relationship between honor codes and academic integrity (McCabe & Trevino, 1997; McCabe, Trevino, & Butterfield, 1999, 2002). Honor codes that are long, formally worded, and include consequences for code violation are linked to higher academic honesty (Gurung, Wilhelm, & Filtz, in press). But having an honor code is not enough. It is necessary to discuss it with students and how it applies to each particular course (Schwartz, Tatum, & Wells, 2012). Faculty should clearly communicate throughout the course that academic integrity is an institutional priority; use some form of written pledge in which students affirm that they have not cheated on a given quiz, discussion post, term paper, or assignment; and encourage students to report any violations of the code they may observe at any point in the course.

## Group Discussions

Engaging students in asynchronous group discussion of key topics or issues on a weekly basis enhances their learning and keeps them connected with each other and with the instructor (Zhang, 2004). In addition, it provides the instructor a documented record of the quality of each student's contribution. Most online software allows the instructor to preserve and archive students' contributions. Rather than simply counting the number of contributions students have made, instructors should provide students with timely feedback with specific comments on the quality of their participation (Jonassen, Lee, Yang, & Laffey, 2005; for examples of rubrics for grading online student participation, see Bartoletti, 2007; Palloff & Pratt, 2003).

Key criteria to be included in a typical guide for evaluating discussion participation include to what extent a learner (a) applies relevant course concepts, theories, or materials correctly; (b) collaborates with fellow learners in relating the discussion to relevant course concepts; (c) applies relevant professional, personal, or other real-world experiences; and (d) supports positions with applicable knowledge (Boettcher & Conrad, 2010).

If participation in online discussion contributes to the course grade, it is important to inform students how their participation in online discussions is graded and to give students feedback regarding the quality and quantity of their participation (Svinicki & McKeachie, 2009). Feedback should be timely, consistent, and specific in recognition of students' low tolerance for delays, ambiguity, and inconsistency in online discussions (Chou, 2001; Jonassen et al., 2005).

## Term Papers

Important differences in implementing writing assignments exist for asynchronous online work. Many online students work full time and/or have family responsibilities; they especially appreciate receiving explicit instructions in advance for all term papers, projects, and assignments when they enroll in the course. These instructions include information regarding learning resources, assessment criteria, grading rubrics, and a timeline for submitting drafts and final version of their papers. To the best of our knowledge, there are no empirical studies concerning the impact of the considerable amount of writing online students do through asynchronous discussions, term papers, and projects. However, a number of authors (see, e.g., Rudestam, 2004) have outlined its potential to make a difference in terms of essential learning outcomes for online students.

## Tests

Traditional forms of testing (e.g., multiple choice, fill in the blank, true/false) are not usually the first choice for determining grades in an online course because of the difficulty in maintaining the integrity of tests. A number of strategies are being explored by online instructors to address the issue of academic integrity.

Computer adaptive testing is one of the sophisticated but promising test security devices for providing unique exams to each learner. The exams are created in real time by the computer using statistical models to present different questions that are based on the student's ability measured in response to previous questions using item response theory (see Kaplan & Saccuzzo, 2009). Typically, a test begins with medium difficulty questions but then tailors itself to each student's achievement level. Because the adaptive testing individualizes the test items a given student is asked to answer, the possibility of cheating is minimized. In addition, the testing time is reduced considerably. However, adaptive testing requires considerable advance planning; instructors need to develop an item bank coded by topic, learning outcome, and level of difficulty. Of course, the initial effort pays off when the computer tailors individualized tests on the basis of students' performance on the preceding items.

Randomization of test items is similar to computer adaptive exams in the sense that a unique set of items is delivered to each learner, but it differs in that no statistical procedure is used to select the items. The key advantage of this approach is that it does not require sophisticated technical support to assemble the item pool; questions are randomly drawn from an item bank to give each student a different set of questions. Collaboration is made difficult when each student's test is markedly different. Most tests are designed to be open book, but once a student begins the test, he or she has a limited amount of time to complete it, and usually only one attempt is allowed. Daniel and Broida (2004) provided a different random selection of test items to each student and found this approach effective in minimizing cheating and improving student learning.

Though not yet empirically tested, the following strategies to minimize the likelihood of cheating have been suggested by Boettcher and Conrad (2010): (a) be clear about the purpose and content of the quizzes you use, (b) set strict time limits for the quizzes, and (c) provide sufficient but low point value. In addition, providing options to retake the quizzes can encourage both competency and self-competition. In sum, use the quizzes for important core concepts, factual knowledge, and beginning concept applications; assign a low point value; and let the course management system do its work after you have created worthwhile and effective quizzes.


## CONCLUSION

In this chapter, we have focused on asynchronous delivery as the most attractive type of online instruction because it provides students with greater control in balancing education, work, and family life. In addition, it makes postsecondary education accessible to learners located in small remote communities where on-campus programs are not available. In preparing this chapter we were guided by two fundamental assumptions: the design of online courses should be based on cognitive theory of how students learn and on empirical evidence concerning features that optimize student learning. Exhibit 4.1 summarizes key empirically based recommendations for teaching online classes. Exhibit 4.2 provides suggestions for future scholarship of teaching and learning on this topic.

## EXHIBIT 4.1
### Evidence-Based Recommendations

- Encourage student self-evaluation and self-regulation by integrating assessment with instruction; ask learners to keep a journal or incorporate other self-monitoring strategies.
- Use technology to embed course goals and objectives, learning resources, assignments, grading policies, and timelines in the syllabus; do not anticipate making significant changes in the syllabus once the course starts.
- Write personable, courteous, and respectful messages to interact with and engage with the students; allocate the amount of time needed to moderate online discussions.
- Select simulations and games that have goals, rules, activities, feedback, and consequences aligned with the stated outcomes of your course.
- Minimize cognitive load by applying appropriate multimedia principles: use relevant visuals and explain them with audio comments; and present explanatory text close to each visual.
- Engage students in active learning—serve as a cognitive guide rather than a dispenser of information.
- Promote academic integrity by using an honor code and discuss with learners how it applies to the online course they are taking with you.
- Promote student–content, student–instructor, and student–student interaction through online discussion groups; provide grading criteria and scoring rubrics in the syllabus; and use them to assess students' contributions in group discussion throughout the course.
- Explore the available options in the learning management system (a) to use multiple methods of assessing student learning and (b) to allow students to track their progress on an ongoing basis.

## EXHIBIT 4.2
### Questions for Future Research

- Why are older students more successful in online courses? Is it prior experience as students or life experiences in general?
- What criteria are most useful in selecting students who have a high probability of completing an online course and achieving the desired outcomes?
- Are students who are collaborative, socially sensitive, self-regulated, and independent likely to be successful learners in conventional campus courses as well as online? Are there factors that distinguish successful online students from their brick-and-mortar campus peers?
- What approaches to presenting information in the syllabus for online courses are particularly effective in facilitating the achievement of learning outcomes?
- To what extent do polished color visuals improve learning and motivation more than simpler formats such as line drawings, tables, and graphic presentations?
- What is the proper role of instructors in online discussions relating to factors such as presenting additional information, providing feedback on posts, generating probes and critical questions, encouraging students to participate, and providing mentoring?

*(continues)*

## EXHIBIT 4.2
### Questions for Future Research  *(Continued)*

- How do the size and composition of the discussion groups affect different learning outcomes? Are groups with similar learners most effective, or should some high-level learners supplant the deficient skills of others?
- How can an online course best support the development of collaborative strategies, self-regulation strategies, and interpersonal skills?
- Does student participation in online discussions improve writing skills? Do deficient writing skills predict dropout rates in courses requiring ongoing participation in group discussions?
- Does the asynchronous learning environment create a more equal opportunity for participation by women and minority students than on-campus courses?
- How can online instructors draw on technological advances to ensure academic integrity in their courses?
- How effective is individualized instruction that dynamically generates learning content on the basis of students' responses? Does this approach lead to increased savings in time and costs for the learners? For the institution?

## REFERENCES

Allen, I. E., & Seaman, J. (2007). *Online nation: Five years of growth in online learning.* Needham, MA: Sloan Consortium.

Althaus, S. (1997). Computer-mediated communication in the university classroom: An experiment with online discussions. *Communication Education, 46,* 158–174. doi:10.1080/03634529709379088

Bartoletti, R. (2007). *Discussion board assignments.* Denton, TX: Texas Woman's University. Retrieved from http://www.twu.edu/downloads/de/discussion_rubric.pdf

Bell, P. D., & Akroyd, D. (2006). Can factors related to self-regulated learning predict learning achievement in undergraduate asynchronous web-based courses? *International Journal of Instructional Technology and Distance Learning, 3*(10). Retrieved from http://itdl.org/index.htm

Betts, K. (2009). Lost in translation: Importance of effective communication in online education. *Online Journal of Distance Learning Administration, 12*(2). Retrieved from http://www.westga.edu/~distance/ojdla/

Bixler, B. A. (2008). *The effects of scaffolding student's problem-solving process via question prompts on problem solving and intrinsic motivation in an online learning environment.* Unpublished doctoral dissertation, Pennsylvania State University, State College.

Blocher, J. M., de Montes, L. S., Willis, E. M., & Tucker, G. (2002). Online-learning: Examining the successful student profile. *The Journal of Interactive Online Learning, 1*(2). Retrieved from http://www.ncolr.org/jiol

Boettcher, J. V., & Conrad, R. M. (2010). *The online teaching survival guide: Simple and practical pedagogical tips.* San Francisco, CA: Jossey-Bass.

Brooks, D. W., Nolan, D. E., & Gallagher, S. J. (2003). Automated testing. *Journal of Science Education and Technology, 12*, 183–186. doi:10.1023/ A:1023943912275

Capella University. (2011). *History of Capella University.* Retrieved from http://www. capella.edu/about_capella/history.aspx

Castaneda, R. 2008. *The impact of computer-based simulation within an instructional sequence on learner performance in a web-based environment.* Unpublished doctoral dissertation, Arizona State University, Tempe.

Chang, M. M. (2007). Enhancing web-based language learning through self-monitoring. *Journal of Computer Assisted Learning, 23*, 187–196. doi:10.1111/ j.1365-2729.2006.00203.x

ChanLin, L. (1998). Animation to teach students of different knowledge levels. *Journal of Instructional Psychology, 25*, 166–175.

Chickering, A. W., & Gamson, Z. F. (1991). Appendix A: Seven principles for good practice in undergraduate education. *New Directions for Teaching and Learning, 1991(47)*, 63–69.

Chou, C. (2001). Formative evaluation of synchronous CMC systems for learner-centered online course. *Journal of Interactive Learning Research, 12*, 173–192.

Chung, S., Chung, M., & Severance, C. (1999, October). *Design of support tools and knowledge building in a virtual university course: Effects of reflection and self-explanation prompts.* Paper presented at WebNet 99 World Conference on the WWW and Internet Proceedings, Honolulu, HI.

Clark, R., & Mayer, R. E. (2008). *E-learning and the science of instruction: Proven guidelines for consumers and designers of multimedia learning* (2nd ed.). San Francisco, CA: Pfeiffer.

Cook, D. A., Dupras, D. M., Thompson, W. G., & Pankratz, V. S. (2005). Web-based learning in residents' continuity clinics: A randomized, controlled trial. *Academic Medicine, 80*, 90–97. doi:10.1097/00001888-200501000-00022

Craig, S. D., Gholson, B., & Driscoll, D. M. (2002). Animated pedagogical agents in multimedia learning environments: Effects of agent properties, picture features, and redundancy. *Journal of Educational Psychology, 94*, 428–434. doi:10.1037/ 0022-0663.94.2.428

Crippen, K. J., & Earl, B. L. (2007). The impact of web-based worked examples and self-explanation on performance, problem solving, and self-efficacy. *Computers & Education, 49*, 809–821. doi:10.1016/j.compedu.2005.11.018

Daniel, D. B., & Broida, J. (2004). Using web-based quizzing to improve exam performance: Lessons learned. *Teaching of Psychology, 31*, 207–208. doi:10.1207/ s15328023top3103_6

Debowski, S., Wood, R., & Bandura, A. (2001). Impact of guided exploration and enactive exploration on self-regulatory mechanisms and information through electronic search. *Journal of Applied Psychology, 86*, 1129–1141. doi:10.1037/ 0021-9010.86.6.1129

Diaz, D. P. (2002). Online drop rates revisited [Commentary]. *The Technology Source* (May/June). Retrieved from http://technologysource.org/

Ebbinghaus, N. (1913). *Memory* (N. R. Ruger & C. E. Bussenius, Trans.). New York, NY: Teacher's College. (Original work published 1885)

Ericsson, K. A. (2006). The influence of experience and deliberate practice on the development of superior expert performance. In K. A. Ericsson, N. Charness, P. J. Feltovich, & R. R. Hoffman (Eds.), *The Cambridge handbook of expertise and expert performance* (pp. 685–706). Cambridge, England: Cambridge University Press.

Ginns, P. (2005). Meta-analysis of the modality effect. *Learning and Instruction, 15,* 313–331. doi:10.1016/j.learninstruc.2005.07.001

Grant, L. K., & Courtoreille, M. (2007). Comparison of fixed-item and response-sensitive versions of an online tutorial. *The Psychological Record, 57,* 265–272.

Gurung, R. A. R., Wilhelm, T., & Filtz, T. (in press). Optimizing honor codes for online test administration. *Ethics & Behavior.*

Hannay, M., & Newvine, T. (2006). Perceptions of distance learning: A comparison of online and traditional learning. *Journal of Online Learning and Teaching, 2*(1). Retrieved from http://jolt.merlot.org/Vol2_No1.htm

Hayes, S. K. (2007). Principles of finance: The design and implementation of an online course. *Journal of Online Learning and Teaching, 2,* 460–465. Retrieved from http://jolt.merlot.org/Vol3_No4.htm

Higher Education Opportunity Act of 2008, Pub. L. No. 110-315, 122 Stat. 3078 (2008).

Hilbelink, A. J. (2007). *The effectiveness and user perception of 3-dimensional digital human anatomy in an online undergraduate anatomy laboratory.* Unpublished doctoral dissertation, University of South Florida, Orlando.

Hrastinski, S. (2008). Asynchronous and synchronous e-learning. *EDUCAUSE Quarterly, 31*(4), 51–55. Retrieved from http://www.educause.edu/eq

Issenberg, S. B., McGaghie, W. C., Petrusa, E. R., Gordon, D. L., & Scalese, R. J. (2005). Features and uses of high fidelity medical simulations that lead to effective learning: A BEME systematic review. *Medical Teacher, 27,* 10–28. doi:10.1080/01421590500046924

Jonassen, D. H., Lee, C. B., Yang, C.-C., & Laffey, J. (2005). The collaboration principle in multimedia learning. In R. E. Mayer (Ed.), *The Cambridge handbook of multimedia learning* (247–270). New York, NY: Cambridge University Press.

Kaplan, R. M., & Saccuzzo, D. P. (2009). *Psychological testing: Principles, applications, and issues* (7th ed.). Belmont, CA: Wadsworth, Cengage Learning.

Liu, S. Y., Gomez, J., & Yen, C. (2009). Community college online course retention and final grade: Predictability of social presence. *Journal of Interactive Online Learning, 8*(2), 165–176. Retrieved from http://www.ncolr.org/jiol/about.html

Mayer, R. E. (1989). Systematic thinking fostered by illustrations in scientific text. *Journal of Educational Psychology, 81,* 240–246. doi:10.1037/0022-0663.81.2.240

Mayer, R. E., & Anderson, R. B. (1991). Animations need narrations: An experimental test of a dual-processing systems in working memory. *Journal of Educational Psychology, 90*, 312–320. doi:10.1037/0022-0663.90.2.312

Mayer, R. E., Dow, G., & Mayer, S. (2003). Multimedia learning in an inter-active self-explaining environment: What works in the design of agent based microworlds? *Journal of Educational Psychology, 95*, 806–812. doi:10.1037/0022-0663.95.4.806

McCabe, D. L., & Trevino, L. K. (1997). Individual and contextual influences on academic dishonesty: A multicampus investigation. *Research in Higher Education, 38*, 379–396. doi:10.1023/A:1024954224675

McCabe, D. L., Trevino, L. K., & Butterfield, K. D. (1999). Academic integrity in honor code and non-honor code environments: A qualitative investigation. *The Journal of Higher Education, 70*, 211–234. doi:10.2307/2649128

McCabe, D. L., Trevino, L. K., & Butterfield, K. D. (2002). Honor codes and other contextual influences on academic integrity. *Research in Higher Education, 43*, 357–378. doi:10.1023/A:1014893102151

Mehrotra, C. M., Hollister, C. D., & McGahey, L. (2001). *Distance learning: Principles for effective design, delivery, and evaluation.* Thousand Oaks, CA: Sage.

Meyer, K. A. (2003). Face-to-face versus threaded discussion: The role of time and higher-order thinking. *Journal of Asynchronous Learning Networks, 7*, 55–65.

Miller, M. V. (2009). Integrating online multimedia into college course and classroom: With application to the social sciences. *Journal of Online Learning and Teaching, 5*, 395–423. Retrieved from http://jolt.merlot.org/Vol5_No2.htm

Moreno, R. (2004). Decreasing cognitive load for novice students: Effects of explanatory versus corrective feedback on discover-based multi-media. *Instructional Science, 32*, 99–113.

Moreno, R., & Mayer, R. E. (1999). Cognitive principles of multimedia learning: The role of modality and contiguity. *Journal of Educational Psychology, 91*, 358–368. doi:10.1037/0022-0663.91.2.358

Moreno, R., & Mayer, R. E. (2002). Learning science in virtual reality multimedia environments: Role of methods and media. *Journal of Educational Psychology, 94*, 598–610. doi:10.1037/0022-0663.94.3.598

Mostyn, G. (2009). An application of contemporary learning theory to online course textbook selection. *The Journal of Online Learning and Teaching, 5*, 649–657. Retrieved from http://jolt.merlot.org/Vol5_No4.htm

Ocker, R. J., & Yaverbaum, G. J. (2001). Collaborative learning environments: Exploring student attitudes and satisfaction in face-to-face and asynchronous computer conferencing settings. *Journal of Interactive Learning Research, 12*, 427–449.

Ollerenshaw, A., Aidman, E., & Kidd, G. (1997). Is an illustration always worth ten thousand words? Effects of prior knowledge, learning style, and multimedia illustrations on text comprehension. *International Journal of Instructional Media, 24*, 227–238.

Palloff, R., & Pratt, K. (2003). *The virtual student.* San Francisco, CA: Jossey-Bass.

Rawson, K. A., & Kintsch, W. (2005). Rereading effects depend on time of test. *Journal of Educational Psychology, 97*, 70–80. doi:10.1037/0022-0663.97.1.70

Rudestam, K. E. (2004). Distributed education and the role of online learning in training professional psychologists. *Professional Psychology: Research and Practice, 35*, 427–432. doi:10.1037/0735-7028.35.4.427

Rudestam, K. E., & Schoenholtz-Read, J. (2002). *Handbook of online learning: Innovations in higher education and corporate training.* Thousand Oaks, CA: Sage.

Saito, H., & Miwa, K. (2007). Construction of a learning environment supporting learners' reflection: A case of information seeking on the web. *Computers & Education, 49*, 214–229. doi:10.1016/j.compedu.2005.07.001

Schwartz, B. M., Tatum, H. E., & Wells, J. W. (2012). The honor code: Influences on attitudes, behaviors, and pedagogy. In R. E. Landrum & M. A. McCarthy (Eds.), *Teaching ethically: Challenges and opportunities.* Washington, DC: American Psychological Association.

Shaw, G. P., & Pieter, W. (2000). The use of asynchronous learning networks in nutrition education: Student attitude, experiences and performance. *Journal of Asynchronous Learning Networks, 4*, 40–51.

Smith, G. G., Ferguson, D., & Caris, M. (2002). Teaching online versus face-to-face. *Journal of Educational Technology Systems, 30*, 337–364. doi:10.2190/FFWX-TJJE-5AFQ-GMFT

Svinicki, M., & McKeachie, W. J. (2009). *McKeachie's teaching tips: Strategies, research, and theory for college and university teachers.* Boston, MA: Houghton-Mifflin.

Tu, C. (2002). The measurement of social presence in an online learning environment. *International Journal on E-Learning, 1*(2), 34–45.

U.S. Department of Education. (2009). *Evaluation of evidence-based practices in online learning: A meta-analysis and review of online learning studies.* Washington, DC: Author.

Uribe, D., Klein, J., & Sullivan, H. (2003). The effect of computer-mediated collaborative learning on solving ill-defined problems. *Educational Technology Research and Development, 51*, 5–19. doi:10.1007/BF02504514

Wang, A. Y., & Newlin, M. H. (2000). Characteristics of students who enroll and succeed in psychology web-based classes. *Journal of Educational Psychology, 92*, 137–143. doi:10.1037/0022-0663.92.1.137

Wiggins, G., & McTighe, J. (2005). *Understanding by design* (Expanded, 2nd ed.). Alexandria, VA: Association for Supervision and Curriculum Development.

Wojciechowski, A., & Palmer, A. B. (2005). Individual student characteristics: Can any be predictors of success in online classes? *Online Journal of Distance Learning Administration, 8*(2). Retrieved from http://www.westga.edu/~distance/ojdla/

Zhang, K. (2004). *Effects of peer-controlled or externally structured and moderated online collaboration on group problem solving processes and related individual attitudes in well-structured and ill-structured small group problem solving in a hybrid course.* Unpublished doctoral dissertation, Pennsylvania State University, University Park.

# 5

# EXPERIENTIAL LEARNING

KRISTIN M. VESPIA, GEORJEANNA WILSON-DOENGES,
RYAN C. MARTIN, AND DEIRDRE M. RADOSEVICH

Experiential learning is not a new concept, but it is one that is frequently misunderstood. From the perspective of Kolb and Kolb (2005), students must in some way transform their experiences for learning to occur. Kolb and Kolb argued that to label an activity *experiential learning*, it is not sufficient for students simply to participate in a group activity (e.g., active learning) or volunteer at a community agency as a part of a course requirement (e.g., service learning); rather, those activities become constructed experiential learning when students reflect on them, develop abstract ideas on the basis of their reflections, and can actively test those ideas. In the pages that follow, we examine a number of popular approaches to experiential learning, such as service learning and research assistantships or apprenticeships. Although the ideas presented in this chapter should be applicable to multiple academic fields and different levels of education, our focus is on education in the psychology discipline and on the undergraduate experience. Experiential learning is key as part of a quality undergraduate education in order to develop psychologically literate students (Dunn, McCarthy, Baker, Halonen, & Hill, 2007; Dunn et al., 2010), and it is a feature of many programs (Stoloff et al., 2009).

# SERVICE LEARNING

Of all the experiential learning techniques that enhance the educational experience of undergraduates, the most extensive literature is on service learning. A meta-analysis of outcomes for service learning illustrated that fields using and publishing about service learning include business management, social work, and education (Conway, Amel, & Gerwien, 2009). Service learning links education with organized service in the community, taking students out of the classroom and into various organizations to meet community needs (Bringle & Hatcher, 1995). This type of socially responsive experience (Bringle & Duffy, 1998) has strong theoretical backing (Kolb & Kolb, 2005; Yates & Youniss, 1996) with empirical evidence for producing positive outcomes, including changes in academic, personal, citizenship, and social variables (Conway et al., 2009).

## Approaches to Service Learning

To be truly considered service learning, the learning experience must be an educational activity for academic credit that meets identified community needs and integrates course material through some type of reflection (Kretchmar, 2001; Lundy, 2007). The amount of direct contact with community members and organizations varies widely. Some bring agency representatives to campus and have the class complete an assignment for the agency without ever setting foot there (Heckert, 2009), whereas others have direct contact with agency constituents for multiple hours weekly over the course of the semester (e.g., Kretchmar, 2001; Lundy, 2007). There is also a great variety in number of hours of service, with some requiring fewer than 10 hours and others requiring more than 40 hours over a semester (Conway et al., 2009).

## Outcomes of Service Learning

Conway et al. (2009) provided a thorough collection of empirical tests of outcomes of service learning across many disciplines. Their meta-analysis of over 100 pre- and postpublished studies demonstrated positive changes for all types of outcomes that were grouped into four categories: academic, personal, social, and citizenship results. Service learning impacted these four sets of outcomes at varying degrees, and, furthermore, the positive effects of service learning were moderated by the amount of structured reflection and curricular (vs. noncurricular) service included in each course. Structured reflection includes activities in which the student ties the service experiences in the field to the learning in the academic setting through some form of mandatory reflection (e.g., a paper or journal). Reflecting about this type of connection increased the positive change in all four outcome categories, with the greatest change in the personal outcome category. In addition, service learning within the educational confines of a class demonstrated more positive outcomes than noncurricular service (e.g., volunteering outside of class).

## Service-Learning Best Practices

From the strong set of empirical results that have been reviewed, the following are suggested best practices for accomplishing service learning as an experiential learning technique.

### Use Structured Reflection

One of the well-documented moderators of service-learning outcomes is structured reflection (Conway et al., 2009). Examples include students keeping a journal to connect their site experience with in-class concepts, having discussions to link service to course content, and incorporating a writing assignment to reflect on a deep question linking course goals to service learning (Bringle & Hatcher, 1999; Lundy, 2007). All forms of reflection, especially if they are designed to maximize course learning and integrate the service with course content, seem to be effective in improving student academic, personal, social, and citizenship outcomes (Conway et al., 2009).

### Incorporate Direct Contact With Clients

Service-learning participants with direct contact scored higher on measures of commitment to others in difficulty and understanding community problems (Kretchmar, 2001). Lundy (2007) found that direct contact with people served was related to higher postproject empathy scores. Direct contact with marginalized populations can help change stereotypical beliefs and attitudes (Conway et al., 2009). If direct contact with clients is not feasible, then contact with agency representatives would be a next-best option to connect students with the population they are serving (Heckert, 2009). However, there are certainly ethical issues to consider when placing undergraduate students in direct contact with clients. Although the benefits of increased empathy and attitude change are clear (Conway et al., 2009; Lundy, 2007), placing students who are unprepared or unable to perform the service-learning requirements in direct contact with clients can be stressful for the student (Kretchmar, 2001) and potentially harmful to the client, as well. More empirical research on ethical concerns involved with service learning is needed.

### Provide Feedback Along the Way

Providing frequent and specific feedback to students from classmates, professors, and even the people served can further increase the benefits of service learning (Heckert, 2009). To ensure feedback is given along the way, dividing the project into smaller subsections that are evaluated throughout the semester and giving students in-class work time may be beneficial to the quality of the project, as well as to the student's experience (Connor-Greene, 2002; Heckert, 2009).

### Create an Autonomy-Supportive Learning Environment

Service learning creates an environment that students perceive as positive and autonomy supportive (Levesque-Bristol & Stanek, 2009). On the basis of self-determination theory, these results support service learning as a teaching tool that impacts student motivation and learning by creating an environment that supports autonomous learning, including choice and ownership, while connecting with faculty and other students (Deci & Ryan, 2000). Best practice would suggest creating an autonomy-supportive service-learning project that includes choice (Levesque-Bristol & Stanek, 2009). Students should be able to choose a project on the basis of information provided before site selection, including a presentation made by the community partner or a community service fair, if possible (Kretchmar, 2001; Levesque-Bristol & Stanek, 2009). Providing experiential activities (e.g., site-based work) and a problem-based learning approach (e.g., having students working on a solution to a problem at the community site) are other effective ways to increase the autonomy-supportive nature of a service-learning course by engaging students with the community organization and helping them develop ownership over solutions.

### Tap Into National Resources

The National Service-Learning Partnership (http://www.service-learningpartnership.org), Youth Service America (http://www.ysa.org), and National Service-Learning Clearinghouse (http://www.servicelearning.org) are excellent resources that provide basic information about getting started, guides for monitoring progress, examples of structured reflection activities, and conferences and contacts for additional networking about service learning (Heckert, 2009).

## INTERNSHIPS

Internships provide students the opportunity to spend several hours in a setting that requires them to do the following: (a) apply knowledge from previous coursework, (b) engage in critical thinking, and (c) reflect on their learning experience (Kiser, 2008). Internships also provide students an opportunity to gain job-related experiences that allow them to be more competitive to potential employers or graduate programs (Gault, Redington, &

Schlager, 2000; Hurst, 2008). By incorporating internships into their curriculum, universities are leveraging the value that can be realized by combining the conceptual learning in the classroom with hands-on learning (Knouse, Tanner, & Harris, 1999). Internships can have many benefits for the student, such as mentorship, networking opportunities, and the ability to gain a deeper understanding of their potential career choice.

## Approaches to Internships

Undergraduate programs have developed various models of internships. Some students are paid for their work, some earn academic credit, and some are able to receive both monetary compensation and academic credit (Baird, 2008). Although undergraduates are limited in the types of psychological services they can provide to the public, numerous programs and professors have developed creative internship experiences (Kay & Rangel, 2009; Weis, 2004). Even with this limitation, there are still opportunities for students to engage in meaningful work with populations who use psychological services. The American Psychological Association (APA; 2010) provides a brief list of internship opportunities available to undergraduate students.

## Outcomes of Internships

Although internships are a frequently used method in undergraduate curriculum, few studies have assessed their effectiveness in relation to experiential learning (Stoloff et al., 2009). In one study, students were found to be more successful in achieving both personal and course-related goals when their internship was well structured (Morris & Haas, 1984). Specifically, students were more successful in their positions when they clearly understood their roles, worked for one boss, and received explicit feedback about their performance and communication process. These findings suggest that students are better able to learn in an internship placement when the expectations are clearly indicated and agreed on by both the professor and the on-site supervisor. Another important piece of the puzzle is reflection as an aspect of the learning process. Authors believe that individual student reflection helps with the integration of theoretical concepts and application of skills (Hascher, Concord, & Moser, 2004). An impressive exemplar of an internship aimed specifically at increasing experiential learning is the Experiential Internship Learning Program (EILP) at Seaver College (Shatzer, 2008). Shatzer (2008) found that components of the EILP impacted learning by improving skills related both to verbal and written communication in addition to general knowledge, and students reported feeling satisfied with their learning experience.

## Best Practices for Internships

Although the empirical literature on internship outcomes is limited, a careful review of that information, as well as other professional writings about internships, suggests that the following approaches would be beneficial in this type of experiential learning.

### Identify Learning Objectives and Responsibilities

Students should be able to tailor their internship to address their individual learning objectives by identifying applied skills they want to develop that will increase their understanding of theoretical concepts presented in course work. As a result, students should develop learning objectives in conjunction with their faculty advisors (Kiser, 2008). Also, the faculty advisor and on-site supervisors should address the interns' specific responsibilities to ensure a clear understanding of what is expected of the student (Morris & Haas, 1984). Faculty should also assess the student's abilities, interpersonal skills, and maturity level prior to internship placement as a means to protect the public and the student from possible ethical issues. In addition, efforts should be made to ensure that the internship supervisor and faculty member provide an opportunity for a meaningful work experience that allows the student to engage in deeper reflection and addresses the identified learning objectives set forth by the student, professor, and internship supervisor.

### Ensure Ongoing Communication About Intern Evaluation

The faculty advisor and on-site supervisor should discuss how the intern will be evaluated and both the frequency and timing of the assessments. It is recommended that interns be evaluated at the midpoint and final stages of the internship experience (Baird, 2008; Kiser, 2008). The feedback should provide suggestions for ongoing adjustments to performance and thoughts on how to further develop the intern's skills (Hascher et al., 2004).

### Include Reflection Papers or Journals/Logs About the Internship Experience

Consistent with other forms of experiential learning, reflection on the internship experience is an important step that facilitates the integrative processing of skills and theoretical concepts (Hascher et al., 2004). Encouraging students to keep a daily journal of the internship experience requires them to reflect on their learning experience instead of passively engaging in applied experiences without making the connection between those experiences and technical or theoretical concepts.

# UNDERGRADUATE TEACHING ASSISTANTSHIPS

Another experiential learning option is student involvement in instruction. Teaching assistants (TAs) at the graduate level are common, and there is an existing literature associated with the practice (e.g., Prieto & Meyers, 1999; Sargent, Allen, Frahm, & Morris, 2009). At the undergraduate level, however, these experiences may be more focused on the TA's learning than on the provision of needed services for the department. Teaching a topic can be an extremely effective method for learning that content (Fremouw, Millard, & Donahoe, 1979). Although more empirical evidence to support the assertions that follow would be helpful, we argue that the undergraduate TA experience may have additional benefits, such as enhancing knowledge of pedagogy and promoting group facilitation, leadership, and public-speaking skills (Boeding & Vattano, 1976; Hogan, Norcross, Cannon, & Karpiak, 2007).

## Approaches to Teaching Assistantships

Undergraduate TAs fill many roles. They may lead discussion sections or sessions (Boeding & Vattano, 1976; White & Kolber, 1978); assist with in-class activities or problem-based learning groups (Hogan et al., 2007; McKeegan, 1998); help with clerical tasks (McKeegan, 1998); provide one-on-one tutoring or feedback on papers (McKeegan, 1998); give a lecture or piece of a lecture (McKeegan, 1998); run review sessions (Hogan et al., 2007); help with grading (Fremouw et al., 1979; McKeegan, 1998); record the completion of assignments but not grade them (Hogan et al., 2007); and even assist with specific skills, such as APA Style or using computerized statistical packages (Hogan et al., 2007). In many instances students receive course credit for their work, but in others students receive no credit and no pay, simply transcript acknowledgement (Hogan et al., 2007). They may also work with introductory courses or with more advanced research methods (McKeegan, 1998), psychological testing, or clinical psychology (Hogan et al., 2007) classes. Of course, having undergraduates in a position of authority over peers and fulfilling the roles just described raises potential ethical or even legal (e.g., compliance with the Family Educational Rights and Privacy Act) questions. Such concerns likely center on (a) the tasks that are appropriate or inappropriate to assign them, (b) the question of whether their use prioritizes TAs' learning at the expense of the overall quality of their peers' educational experience, and (c) the potential for the TAs themselves to be exploited to reduce faculty workload.

## Outcomes of Teaching Assistantships

Much of the undergraduate TA literature is descriptive and does not directly address all of the ethical concerns or potential roles that TAs fill.

It instead emphasizes the examination of models for TA use or the report of student and faculty perceptions of learning from the TA experience. Existing studies on the outcomes of serving as a TA demonstrate an increase in self-confidence and stronger connections with one's major (Weidert, Roethel, & Gurung, 2010) and better understanding of the experience of being a teacher, together with improved library research and APA Style skills, awareness of their own limitations, and more effective work with individuals from other cultures (McKeegan, 1998). Other benefits could include graduate school preparation and competitiveness for assistantships (McKeegan, 1998), obtaining relevant career information (Hogan et al., 2007), and increased confidence (Boeding & Vattano, 1976). Interestingly, TAs who regularly and formally reflected on their TA work (i.e., in a journal) were significantly more likely to go on to graduate-level education than those who did not (Weidert et al., 2010). Looking beyond self-report, a pre- and posttest experimental examination of the effects of serving as an undergraduate TA demonstrated that TAs significantly outperformed a control group of psychology majors on the final exam, illustrating they had learned course content as a part of the TA experience (controlling for pretest scores and GPA; Fremouw et al., 1979, p. 31). Undergraduate TAs were even rated significantly more helpful than the graduate assistants (Fremouw et al., 1979, p. 32), consistent with the findings of White and Kolber (1978), who also discovered that students gave significantly higher ratings to undergraduate TAs when compared with graduate TAs.

## Teaching Assistantship Best Practices

The existing literature on teaching assistantships also lends itself to the identification of a series of recommendations for ensuring that they become true experiential learning activities for undergraduates. These recommendations share much in common with those already described for service learning and internships.

### Have Formal Selection and Training Procedures

TAs should be carefully selected and trained to ensure that they possess appropriate knowledge and skills, as well as the maturity necessary for leading their peers. Training is endorsed by undergraduate faculty who use TAs (e.g., Hogan et al., 2007; McKeegan, 1998) and in the literature, including the association between training for graduate TAs and greater teaching self-efficacy (Prieto & Meyers, 1999). Hogan et al. (2007) described a one-credit seminar for preparing undergraduate TAs and the topics included (e.g., encouraging discussion, evaluating learning). They noted that the topics rated by TAs as having the greatest learning value were teaching ethics, problem-based learning, and performing item analysis.

*Be Clear About Roles, Expectations, and Learning Outcomes*

McKeegan (1998) described having a contract with TAs that explains her role and tasks, along with those of the TA. Clearly defining roles and expectations may help students to understand both what they are to learn and how to achieve those objectives. Establishing and evaluating specific learning outcomes will help maintain a focus on the TA's education and address some potential ethical concerns.

*Incorporate Structured Reflection Activities*

Although based on a very small sample, Weidert et al.'s (2010) findings suggested that structured reflection on the TA experience is related to positive outcomes. Having students maintain a journal or engage in systematic discussions about what they are learning may promote additional growth.

*Consider a TA Team*

Given that students are entering an unfamiliar role and that they report learning from interactions with other TAs (McKeegan, 1998), having more than one TA for a class or having TAs for multiple classes/sections meet together for ongoing training or reflection may enhance the learning experience.

## CONDUCTING AND PARTICIPATING IN RESEARCH AS EXPERIENTIAL LEARNING

Undergraduate TAs are a relatively recent phenomenon, and when faculty members think about experiential learning opportunities, service learning and internships probably come to mind most readily because of the community connections they clearly conjure. Another form of experiential learning is clearly related to one of the core learning objectives of psychology curricula, research methods (APA, 2007).

### Approaches to and Outcomes of Conducting and Participating in Research

Two of the common manners in which undergraduates are exposed to psychological research are through serving as participants in empirical studies themselves and through actually conducting research. Both of these experiences are likely to occur within the context of an existing class.

## Student Participation in Research

Psychology instructors work to help students experience the research process in many different ways. Arguably the most common mechanism for exposing students to the research process, with 33% of undergraduate degree-granting institutions (Landrum & Chastain, 1999) and 74% of graduate degree-granting institutions (Sieber & Saks, 1989) having one, is the departmental participant pool, which is also a potential experiential learning tool. Interestingly, there are few empirical studies on the learning value of participant pools, and the results of such studies are mixed. Although some have found that mandating research participation leads to the devaluation of psychology and psychological research (Nimmer & Handelsman, 1992), others have found that participation improves understanding of ethical research practices (Rosell et al., 2005) and is associated with more positive perceptions of psychology (Bowman & Waite, 2003) and a better understanding of themselves or the research content area (Wilson-Doenges & Martin, 2008).

## Student-Conducted Research in the Classroom

Looking beyond research participation, one of the primary ways students can learn about research is through conducting an in-class research project, another potential method of experiential learning. Educators have established that such in-class projects help students recognize the relevance of the research (Saville, 2008), and because the scientific method is considered a core element of the psychological discipline (Dunn et al., 2010), having students complete a research project as part of their academic career makes intuitive sense.

There is a substantial literature base outlining different approaches to structuring in-class research projects (Chapdelaine & Chapman, 1999; Marek, Christopher, & Walker, 2004; Saville, 2008; Wiggins & Burns, 2009). Several authors have recognized the logistical difficulties associated with organizing multiple student research projects in a given semester and outlined strategies to help. For example, Marek et al. (2004) suggested selecting a theme on which all the projects and assignments are based to help address time and resource constraints. Likewise, Saville (2008) recommended using "canned" projects that have already been developed by the instructor before the class begins. These authors acknowledged, though, that there are problems with these approaches in that they decrease input from and, potentially, motivation of students, and students miss important aspects of research development (e.g., formulating a research question, conducting a thorough literature review; Marek et al., 2004; Saville, 2008).

In-class research projects sometimes lead students to approach this class with greater trepidation than many of their other courses (Schober, Wagner, Reimann, Atria, & Spiel, 2006). To address this reticence, a significant literature base has suggested that working on problem-based or community-based research projects will provide a context for the research and will increase motivation (Chapdelaine & Chapman, 1999; Wiggins & Burns, 2009). Chapdelaine and Chapman (1999) suggested collaborating with a community agency to design a research project that will have real-life implications for the agency. With these sorts of external agency collaborations, students have another opportunity, beyond professional conferences, to present their results and to see the direct impact of their projects.

## Best Practices for Exposing Students to Research in the Classroom

Both conducting and participating in research are potentially powerful forms of experiential learning. Faculty members should be aware of some of the specific strategies that could enhance the quality of those learning experiences.

### Encourage Early Involvement

The scientific method is at the core of the psychological discipline (Dunn et al., 2010). Requiring students to take research methods and to complete their first, and maybe only, research project early in their career sets them up for a better understanding of later material. Similarly, serving as a research participant during their introductory course exposes them to the nuts and bolts of the scientific method as it applies to psychology.

### Offer Structure

Because the investigative process can be overwhelming for new researchers, it is helpful to offer structure regarding their projects. By giving them guidelines as to the method they must use, the participants with whom they must work, and the statistical analyses they should conduct, the instructor may alleviate some of that anxiety without watering down the process by doing too much of the work for them. However, the value of structured versus unstructured research projects has not yet been tested and should be the focus of future research.

### Work to Provide a Context

Consistent with the literature described earlier (Chapdelaine & Chapman, 1999; Wiggins & Burns, 2009), helping students see the real-world application for their research may help to increase their motivation and their ownership of the projects.

*Encourage Reflection*

As has been found with service learning, internships, and TAs, students' learning may be enhanced when they are encouraged to be reflective about their experience (e.g., Conway et al., 2009). Whether serving as a research participant, completing a research proposal, or conducting a full research study, students should be encouraged to reflect on their work throughout the process. Having them keep a research methods journal or write reflection essays will help them think about what they are learning throughout the semester.

*Be Sensitive to Ethical Issues*

There are potential ethical issues associated with both having students serve as research participants and having students conduct research, and instructors must be sensitive to such issues. It is important for instructors to be aware of relevant institutional review board (IRB) policies and relevant APA ethical guidelines regarding such research.

*Make Sure the Requirement is Manageable, Provide Options, and Assess*

Students learn most from participating in research when (a) the amount of research participation required is manageable, (b) alternative and comparable options are available, and (c) they are provided feedback about the purpose and results of the research (Landrum & Chastain, 1999; Sieber, 1999). Instructors have the ethical responsibility to offer alternatives to research participation, and although the standard alternative option is to have students review research articles (Landrum & Chastain, 1999), offering a broader array of alternatives can facilitate learning. For example, students could attend faculty/student research presentations or researcher panel discussions as possible alternatives. Finally, one thing that is evident from the research on participant pools (Bowman & Waite, 2003; Nimmer & Handelsman, 1992; Rosell et al., 2005; Wilson-Doenges & Martin, 2008) is the false perception that learning is automatic for student participants, meaning that each institution should determine the educational value, if any, of the participant pool. This finding is perhaps consistent with the theoretical arguments about experiential learning in general, which would suggest that simply participating in an activity is not sufficient for learning to occur (Kolb & Kolb, 2005).

# UNDERGRADUATE RESEARCH ASSISTANTSHIPS

Another increasingly popular experiential learning opportunity is the undergraduate research assistantship (RA). Such experiences are particularly common in large psychology departments, in the natural and physical sciences (Kardash, 2000), and in teaching-focused institutions (Starke, 1985; Szuchman, 2006). RAs have been discussed in the literature for decades (e.g., Evans, Rintala, Guthrie, & Raines, 1981; Wayment & Dickson, 2008), and Perlman and McCann (2005) reported that 65% of psychology departments in their national survey offered undergraduate RA positions with faculty members, with 27% providing opportunities to work with graduate students. The popularity of such experiences can also be seen in the development of the Council on Undergraduate Research and its corresponding journal (Hogan et al., 2007).

## Approaches to Research Assistantships

RA opportunities have become common and are implemented a number of different ways. The opportunity may involve pay (Szuchman, 2006) or academic credit (Gibson, Kahn, & Mathie, 1996), or it may simply be a volunteer position (Plante, 1998). Students may work in an individual mentoring relationship or as part of a larger research team; they may work for one semester or be asked to make a multiple-term commitment (Landrum & Nelsen, 2002).

Several RA models have been described formally, although undoubtedly more exist. Gibson et al. (1996) discussed two approaches, one in which a faculty member and students worked on a single project, but in which that faculty member was responsible for the individual learning goals, training, and work of each undergraduate. The second model involved three faculty members and many more students working on multiple related projects, either with all members playing some role in all projects or with smaller subgroups focusing on one ongoing study. Plante (1998) used a laboratory model. He worked with students on multiple studies and conducted lab meetings with weekly discussions of each project. Within that general format, however, some students spent relatively little time involved in research with only basic responsibilities, whereas others became student managers for individual studies, which typically included mentoring other students and even research writing under supervision. Szuchman (2006), by contrast, involved multiple undergraduates in one grant-funded study but held no lab meetings, relying on individual training methods. Jones and Draheim (1994) described yet another model in which one faculty member and one student worked together intensively as the professor wrote a textbook. Finally, the National Science Foundation funds Research Experiences for Undergraduates programs, and these can involve paid stipends to spend weeks of a summer at a host institution, formal academic seminars, and opportunities for students to create their own studies under the mentorship of a faculty member (Page, Abramson, & Jacobs-Lawson, 2004). Faculty members could also offer traditional RAs to their students during the summer, when they and the students may have more time to focus on scholarship (Tatum & Schwartz, 2008).

## Outcomes of Research Assistantships

Formal evaluation of RA outcomes has tended to rely on faculty and student self-report. On the basis of faculty responses, Landrum and Nelsen (2002) reported two major classes of RA benefits: skill-based (e.g., data analysis, writing ability) and interpersonal (e.g., teamwork, getting to know faculty members). Kierniesky (2005) described other faculty-perceived benefits of undergraduate research, including increased psychological knowledge, research and critical thinking skills, personal development, graduate school preparation, and enhanced faculty productivity and student–faculty relationships (Plante, 1998). Students' reports about the RA experience further included increased knowledge in the field or about specific topics, such as research methods and ethics (Gibson et al., 1996; Jones & Draheim, 1994; Kardash, 2000; Starke, 1985). Students also noted improved skills, such as those for library research, collecting and analyzing data, writing, using computers, critical thinking, time management, public speaking, self-confidence, and working in a team (Gibson et al., 1996; Jones & Draheim, 1994; Kardash, 2000). Finally, students reported positive feelings about being an RA (Evans, Rintala, Guthrie, & Raines, 1981), the acquisition of transferable skills (Evans et al., 1981; Starke, 1985), and increased consideration of career options (Jones & Draheim, 1994).

## Research Assistantship Best Practices

The recommendations that follow for maximizing the potential of the RA as an experiential learning tool are based on the empirical findings and professional writings already described for this type of activity. Again, common themes with the best practices for service learning, teaching assistantships, and other learning opportunities outlined in this chapter are readily apparent.

### Have an Application or Screening Process

Several authors have described selection processes and criteria, whether standard for the department or individualized (Jones & Draheim, 1994; Plante, 1998; Szuchman, 2006; Wayment & Dickson, 2008), for choosing RAs. Having some type of formal application and screening process benefits students and faculty by ensuring a good fit between RAs, professors, and specific projects, as well as making these opportunities more widely known (Jones & Draheim, 1994; Wayment & Dickson, 2008).

### Provide Formal Training for RAs

Training may involve group sessions or one-on-one mentoring (e.g., Gibson et al., 1996; Plante, 1998; Szuchman, 2006). Research ethics and the role of IRBs may be particularly important to review, given their educational value and importance to the well-being of research participants. As with other experiential learning opportunities, potential ethical concerns can be raised about the nature and extent of undergraduates' involvement in research. One helpful tool for preventing such concerns could be the online research ethics modules that are required by many institutions and their IRB review process.

### Establish and Assess Learning Outcomes

Gibson et al. (1996) described having students develop a learning plan that outlines their existing research skills, along with the skills they want to learn as an RA. Formal articulation of such goals may help focus both faculty members and students on the RA as a learning experience (Gibson et al., 1996). Assessing the achievement of those goals in a tangible way (e.g., testing research knowledge, tracking the number of student coauthorships) could help faculty members evaluate the assistantship.

### Offer Multiple-Semester Experiences

Given the plethora of skills that could be potential outcomes of the RA and the dynamic nature of research, students may need to work for more than one semester to obtain a thorough learning experience. Landrum and Nelsen (2002) noted that some faculty members ask for 2-year commitments from RAs.

### Provide Opportunities for Reflection

Students may experience interpersonal benefits from the RA experience (Landrum & Nelsen, 2002), including team building or changes in graduate school plans. Although the potential benefits have been evaluated in the literature reviewed, asking students to reflect on what they are learning and how they are reacting to the RA experience may increase student awareness of such outcomes.

### Consider Departmental Coordination

Wayment and Dickson (2008) described a process that dramatically increased student and faculty participation in undergraduate research activities. For example, they created a standard application and application deadline for RAs, advertised faculty research interests and the application process in multiple venues, highlighted student RAs in their department newsletter, and provided one course reassignment to professors who were very involved in scholarly activities.

*Be Aware of the Ethics Involved in Mentoring Relationships*

Ethics are not limited to interactions with research participants and materials. Faculty members may develop close relationships with RAs, and that may facilitate the research process. Professors must be aware of the power they hold and the potential risks of dual relationships or exploitation (Jones & Draheim, 1994). Faculty members should be particularly cognizant of ethical responsibilities, such as appropriately dealing with authorship credit with students (Plante, 1998). A syllabus or contract that clearly spells out the expectations of both professor and student could help to avoid such problems.

## CONCLUSION

Several themes emerge from the recommendations described in this chapter regarding specific types of experiential learning. Exhibit 5.1 summarizes the empirically based best practices for experiential learning techniques that are based on the existing scholarship of teaching and learning. Despite the need for additional research (see Exhibit 5.2), existing work does clearly reinforce that mere participation in experience does not constitute learning. Attending to best practices—such as the systematic evaluation of outcomes and the thoughtful incorporation of training, learning objectives, and reflection—is critical as educators move from providing their students with experience to facilitating students' experiential learning.

### EXHIBIT 5.1
#### Evidence-Based Recommendations

- Have established application, selection, and training procedures.
- Be explicit about learning objectives, responsibilities, and appropriate roles for participants (e.g., avoid dual relationships, work within the boundaries of one's training and competence).
- Incorporate structured reflection (e.g., journals), feedback on performance, and integration of academic content in the experience, recognizing that mere engagement in activities does not constitute experiential learning.
- Consider the benefits of cooperative or peer learning that may occur through the use of team (e.g., teaching assistantships, research assistantships) or course-embedded (e.g., service learning) experiential opportunities.
- Be cognizant of specific ethical concerns raised by different types of experiential learning, and structure experiences to try to circumvent potential problems. Many of the best practices mentioned could be effective prevention strategies in avoiding ethical quandaries (e.g., formal selection and training procedures; being specific about roles, responsibilities, and learning outcomes).

# EXHIBIT 5.2
## Questions for Future Research

- How do experiential learning outcomes compare with existing benchmarks for educational success in one's field, such as the American Psychological Association's (2007) undergraduate major guidelines?
- What are the concrete, measurable outcomes of experiential learning (e.g., actual knowledge or skill gains rather than student or instructor perceptions; tangible outcomes such as publications, graduate-school admissions, and success in obtaining employment)?
- How do different approaches to experiential learning compare with each other in terms of effectiveness?
- What are the long-term outcomes of service learning? (The immediate outcomes of this technique are already heavily researched.)
- What are the immediate and long-term outcomes of teaching assistantships, research assistantships, and conducting and participating in research?
- What potential ethical concerns are raised by experiential learning, and how effectively do preventive strategies address these concerns?

# REFERENCES

American Psychological Association. (2007). *APA guidelines for the undergraduate psychology major*. Washington, DC: Author. Retrieved from http://www.apa.org/ed/precollege/about/psymajor-guidelines.pdf

American Psychological Association. (2010). *Undergraduate research opportunities and internships*. Retrieved from http://www.apa.org/education/undergrad/research-opps.aspx

Baird, B. N. (2008). *The internship, practicum, and field placement handbook: A guide for the helping professions*. Saddle Brook, NJ: Prentice Hall.

Boeding, C. H., & Vattano, F. J. (1976). Undergraduates as teaching assistants: A comparison of two discussion methods. *Teaching of Psychology, 3*, 55–59. doi:10.1207/s15328023top0302_2

Bowman, L. L., & Waite, B. M. (2003). Volunteering in research: Student satisfaction and educational benefits. *Teaching of Psychology, 30*, 102–106. doi:10.1207/S15328023TOP3002_03

Bringle, R. G., & Duffy, D. K. (1998). *With service in mind: Concepts and models for service-learning in psychology*. Washington, DC: American Association for Higher Education.

Bringle, R. G., & Hatcher, J. A. (1995). A service learning curriculum for faculty. *The Michigan Journal of Community Service Learning, 2*, 112–122.

Bringle, R. G., & Hatcher, J. A. (1999). Reflection in service learning: Making meaning of experience. *Educational Horizons, 77*, 179–185.

Chapdelaine, A., & Chapman, B. L. (1999). Using community-based research projects to teach research methods. *Teaching of Psychology, 26*, 101–105. doi:10.1207/s15328023top2602_4

Connor-Greene, P. A. (2002). Problem-based service learning: The evolution of a team project. *Teaching of Psychology, 29,* 193–197. doi:10.1207/S15328023TOP2903_02

Conway, J. M., Amel, E. L., & Gerwien, D. P. (2009). Teaching and learning in the social context: A meta-analysis of service learning's effects on academic, personal, social and citizenship outcomes. *Teaching of Psychology, 36,* 233–245. doi:10.1080/00986280903172969

Deci, E. L., & Ryan, R. M. (2000). The "what" and "why" of goal pursuits: Human needs and the self-determination of behavior. *Psychological Inquiry, 11,* 227–268. doi:10.1207/S15327965PLI1104_01

Dunn, D. S., Brewer, C. L., Cautin, R. L., Gurung, R. A. R., Keith, K. D., McGregor, L. N., & Voigt, M. J. (2010). The undergraduate psychology curriculum: Call for a core. In D. F. Halpern (Ed.), *Undergraduate education in psychology: A blueprint for the future of the discipline* (pp. 47–61). Washington, DC: American Psychological Association. doi:10.1037/12063-003

Dunn, D. S., McCarthy, M. A., Baker, S., Halonen, J. S., & Hill, W. H., IV. (2007). Quality benchmarks in undergraduate psychology programs. *American Psychologist, 62,* 650–670. doi:10.1037/0003-066X.62.7.650

Evans, R. I., Rintala, D. H., Guthrie, T. J., & Raines, B. E. (1981). Recruiting and training undergraduate psychology research assistants for longitudinal field investigations. *Teaching of Psychology, 8,* 97–100. doi:10.1207/s15328023top0802_9

Fremouw, W. J., Millard, W. J., & Donahoe, J. W. (1979). Learning-through-teaching: Knowledge changes in undergraduate teaching assistants. *Teaching of Psychology, 6,* 30–32. doi:10.1207/s15328023top0601_10

Gault, J., Redington, J., & Schlager, T. (2000). Undergraduate business internships and career success: Are they related? *Journal of Marketing Education, 22,* 45–53. doi:10.1177/0273475300221006

Gibson, P. R., Kahn, A. S., & Mathie, V. A. (1996). Undergraduate research groups: Two models. *Teaching of Psychology, 23,* 36–38. doi:10.1207/s15328023top2301_7

Hascher, T., Concord, Y., & Moser, P. (2004). Forget about theory—practice is all? Student teachers' learning in practicum. *Teachers and Teaching: Theory and Practice, 10,* 623–637. doi:10.1080/1354060042000304800

Heckert, T. M. (2009). Alternative service learning approaches: Two techniques that accommodate faculty schedules. *Teaching of Psychology, 37,* 32–35. doi:10.1080/00986280903175681

Hogan, T. P., Norcross, J. C., Cannon, T., & Karpiak, C. P. (2007). Working with and training undergraduates as teaching assistants. *Teaching of Psychology, 34,* 187–190. doi:10.1080/00986280701498608

Hurst, J. L. (2008). Factors involved in increasing conversion rates of interns into full-time employees. *Dissertation Abstracts International, 68* (9-A), 3949.

Jones, J. L., & Draheim, M. M. (1994). Mutual benefits: Undergraduate assistance in faculty scholarship. *Journal on Excellence in College Teaching, 5,* 85–96.

Kardash, C. M. (2000). Evaluation of an undergraduate research experience: Perceptions of undergraduate interns and their faculty mentors. *Journal of Educational Psychology, 92,* 191–201. doi:10.1037/0022-0663.92.1.191

Kay, T. S., & Rangel, D. K. (2009). National depression screening day: An undergraduate practicum experience. *Teaching of Psychology, 36,* 126–129. doi:10.1080/00986280902739529

Kierniesky, N. C. (2005). Undergraduate research in small psychology departments: Two decades later. *Teaching of Psychology, 32,* 84–90. doi:10.1207/s15328023top3202_1

Kiser, P. M. (2008). *The human services internship: Getting the most from your experience* (2nd ed.). Belmont, CA: Thomson.

Knouse, S. B., Tanner, J. T., & Harris, E. W. (1999). The relation of college internships, college performance, and subsequent job opportunity. *Journal of Employment Counseling, 36,* 35–43.

Kolb, A. Y., & Kolb, D. A. (2005). Learning styles and learning spaces: Enhancing experiential learning in higher education. *Academy of Management Learning & Education, 4,* 193–212. doi:10.5465/AMLE.2005.17268566

Kretchmar, M. D. (2001). Service learning in a general psychology class: Description, preliminary evaluation, and recommendations. *Teaching of Psychology, 28,* 5–10. doi:10.1207/S15328023TOP2801_02

Landrum, R. E., & Chastain, E. (1999). Subject pool policies in undergraduate-only departments: Results from a nationwide survey. In R. E. Landrum & E. Chastain (Eds.), *Protecting human subjects* (pp. 25–42). Washington, DC: American Psychological Association.

Landrum, R. E., & Nelsen, L. R. (2002). The undergraduate research assistantship: An analysis of the benefits. *Teaching of Psychology, 29,* 15–19. doi:10.1207/S15328023TOP2901_04

Levesque-Bristol, C., & Stanek, L. R. (2009). Examining self-determination in a service learning course. *Teaching of Psychology, 36,* 262–266. doi:10.1080/00986280903175707

Lundy, B. L. (2007). Service learning in life-span developmental psychology: Higher exam scores and increased empathy. *Teaching of Psychology, 34,* 23–27. doi:10.1207/s15328023top3401_5

Marek, P., Christopher, A. N., & Walker, B. J. (2004). Learning by doing: Research methods with a theme. *Teaching of Psychology, 31,* 128–131.

McKeegan, P. (1998). Using undergraduate teaching assistants in a research methodology course. *Teaching of Psychology, 25,* 11–14. doi:10.1207/s15328023top2501_4

Morris, S. B., & Haas, L. J. (1984). Evaluating undergraduate field placements: An empirical approach. *Teaching of Psychology, 11,* 166–168.

Nimmer, J. G., & Handelsman, M. M. (1992). Effects of subject pool policy on student attitudes toward psychology and psychological research. *Teaching of Psychology, 19,* 141–144. doi:10.1207/s15328023top1903_2

Page, M. C., Abramson, C. I., & Jacobs-Lawson, J. M. (2004). The National Science Foundation Research Experiences for Undergraduates Program: Experiences and recommendations. *Teaching of Psychology, 31,* 241–247. doi:10.1207/s15328023top3104_3

Perlman, B., & McCann, L. I. (2005). Undergraduate research experiences in psychology: A national study of courses and curricula. *Teaching of Psychology, 32,* 5–14. doi:10.1207/s15328023top3201_2

Plante, T.G. (1998). A laboratory group model for engaging undergraduates in faculty research. *Teaching of Psychology, 25,* 128–130. doi:10.1207/s15328023top2502_13

Prieto, L. R., & Meyers, S. A. (1999). Effects of training and supervision on the self-efficacy of psychology graduate teaching assistants. *Teaching of Psychology, 26,* 264–266. doi:10.1207/S15328023TOP260404

Rosell, M. C., Beck, D. M., Luther, K. E., Goedert, K. M., Shore, W. J., & Anderson, D.D. (2005). The pedagogical value of experimental participation paired with course content. *Teaching of Psychology, 32,* 95–99. doi:10.1207/s15328023top3202_3

Sargent, L. D., Allen, B. C., Frahm, J. A., & Morris, G. (2009). Enhancing the experience of student teams in large classes: Training teaching assistants to be coaches. *Journal of Management Education, 33,* 526–552. doi:10.1177/1052562909334092

Saville, B. K. (2008). *A guide to teaching research methods in psychology.* Malden, MA: Blackwell.

Schober, B., Wagner, P., Reimann, R., Atria, M., & Spiel, C. (2006). Teaching research methods in an internet-based blended-learning setting: Vienna e-lecturing. *Methodology: European Journal of Research Methods for the Behavioral and Social Sciences, 2,* 73–82. doi:10.1027/1614-2241.2.2.73

Shatzer, N. S. (2008). *Liberal arts experiential internship learning and assessment* (Doctoral dissertation). Available from ProQuest Dissertations and Thesis database. (UMI No. 1490082251)

Sieber, J. E. (1999). What makes a subject pool (un)ethical? In R. E. Landrum & E. Chastain (Eds.), *Protecting human subjects* (pp. 43–64). Washington, DC: American Psychological Association.

Sieber, J. E., & Saks, M. J. (1989). A census of subject pool characteristics and qualities. *American Psychologist, 44,* 1053–1061. doi:10.1037/0003-066X.44.7.1053

Starke, M. C. (1985). A research practicum: Undergraduates as assistants in psychological research. *Teaching of Psychology, 12,* 158–160. doi:10.1207/s15328023top1203_12

Stoloff, M., McCarthy, M., Keller, L., Varfolomeeva, V., Lynch, J., Makara, K., ... Smiley, W. (2009). The undergraduate psychology major: An examination of structure and sequence. *Teaching of Psychology, 37,* 4–15. doi:10.1080/00986280903426274

Szuchman, L. T. (2006). Aging research with students in a university with a strong teaching mission. *Educational Gerontology, 32*, 527–538. doi:10.1080/03601270 600723726

Tatum, H., & Schwartz, B. (2008). Summer research programs. In R. L. Miller, R. F. Rycek, E. Balcetis, S. Barney, B. Beins, S. Burns, R. Smith, & M. E. Ware (Eds.), *Developing, promoting and sustaining the undergraduate research experience in psychology* (pp. 140–142). Syracuse, NY: Society for the Teaching of Psychology. Available at http://teachpsych.org/ebooks/ur2008/index.php

Wayment, H. A., & Dickson, K. L. (2008). Increasing student participation in undergraduate research benefits students, faculty, and department. *Teaching of Psychology, 35*, 194–197. doi:10.1080/00986280802189213

Weidert, J., Roethel, A., & Gurung, R. A. R. (2010, August). Benefits of being a UTA: Hard data and critical reflections. In R. A. R. Gurung (Chair), *Best practices for training and using undergraduate teaching assistants.* Symposium conducted at the 118th annual meeting of the American Psychological Association, San Diego, CA.

Weis, R. (2004). Using an undergraduate human-service practicum to promote unified psychology. *Teaching of Psychology, 31*, 43–46.

White, K. M., & Kolber, R. G. (1978). Undergraduate and graduate students as discussion section leaders. *Teaching of Psychology, 5*, 6–9. doi:10.1207/s15328023 top0501_2

Wiggins, S., & Burns, V. (2009). Research methods in practice: The development of problem-based learning materials for teaching qualitative research methods to undergraduate students. *Psychology Learning & Teaching, 8*, 29–33. doi:10.2304/ plat.2009.8.1.29

Wilson-Doenges, G., & Martin, R. C. (2008, August). *What do students really learn from mandatory participant pools?* Poster session presented at the 116th annual meeting of the American Psychological Association, Boston, MA.

Yates, M., & Youniss, J. (1996). A developmental perspective on community service in adolescence. *Social Development, 5*, 85–111. doi:10.1111/j.1467-9507.1996. tb00073.x

# 6

# HOW SHOULD STUDENTS STUDY?

REGAN A. R. GURUNG AND LEE I. McCANN

Students who are getting less than satisfactory grades frequently say they study hard, can describe a variety of time-consuming study activities that are not working well for them, and then ask their instructors what they can do to improve their grades. Some of the many study techniques recommended to students by instructors include "read your textbook and assignments before coming to class" and "take good notes and test yourself often." Some textbooks have suggestions for how to do well in a course, and there are also a number of student study guides (e.g., Fry, 2004; Tamblin & Ward, 2006). But what does the research literature say about study skills? What works? In this chapter, we provide instructors with a review of the empirical evidence on study skills, offer instructors key suggestions to modify their pedagogy to aid student studying, and conclude with items for future research.

## WHY SHOULD FACULTY CARE?

The answer to this question may not be as obvious as it seems. College faculty may believe that students should have picked up good studying skills in high school or that it is the role of academic staff on campus and first-year programs to deliver such training (Gurung & Wilson-Doenges, 2010). Why should instructors be paying attention to how their students are studying? It is now clear that good study behaviors predict academic success (Credé & Kuncel, 2008; Hattie, 2009; Prevatt, Petscher, Proctor, Hurst, & Adams, 2006). In fact, study behaviors predict academic performance over and above standardized tests and previous grades (e.g., high school GPA; Credé & Kuncel, 2008). Credé and Kuncel (2008) conducted a meta-analysis of 344 studies examining the construct and predictive validity of 10 study-skill constructs for college students. They found that study behaviors showed "substantial incremental validity" (p. 425) in predicting first-year student GPA. Of note, they also found study behaviors to be only moderately related to study skills ($\rho = .27$). These findings make it clear that study behaviors play a critical role in determining student success, and faculty need to take heed. Hattie (2009) conducted a meta-analysis of 800 meta-analyses over 15,000 studies and found that interventions to improve study skills were significant in improving learning, with effect sizes ranging from 0.59 (for teaching study skills) to 0.71 (for spaced vs. mass practice) and 0.69 (for metacognitive strategies), significantly above the average effect sizes found (0.40).

## WHAT EXACTLY ARE STUDY BEHAVIORS?

*Study behaviors* can be broadly defined as behaviors serving to acquire, organize, synthesize, evaluate, remember, and use information (Gettinger & Seibert, 2002). Such behaviors include goal setting; selecting what, how, and where to study; taking good notes; reading; and self-testing. A review of the research on study behaviors showed the existence of three major areas: (a) study habits, skills, and attitudes; (b) information processing during studying; and (c) metacognitive skills (Credé & Kuncel, 2008; Hacker, Dunlosky, & Graesser, 2009). *Study skills* refer to the student's knowledge of strategies and methods, including the ability to manage time. *Study habits* refer to the engagement in study behaviors (e.g., memorization). *Study attitudes* refer to the student's attitude toward the act of studying and "acceptance and approval of the broader goals of a college education" (Credé & Kuncel, 2008, p. 427). Informational processing approaches examined the level of processing of information. *Deep* processing is said to occur when students relate new knowledge to existing knowledge and otherwise manipulate what they are learning (e.g., apply, evaluate, synthesize). In contrast, students taking a *surface* approach primarily use rote memorization (Entwistle, 2009; Marton & Saljo, 1976).

Over the years, study behaviors have been operationalized and measured in different ways. Some researchers have used measurement items to separate the high-scoring student from the low-scoring student (Brown & Holtzman, 1955). Others have based measures of study behaviors on a more theoretical basis using information-processing approaches (see Entwistle, 2009). Still other researchers have derived measures from the ground up after observing student behavior (Gurung, Weidert, & Jeske, 2010). Consequently, there are many different ways to measure study behaviors, a topic we turn to next.

## MAIN MEASURES OF STUDY BEHAVIORS

Measures of study behaviors, also called study skills, strategies, or techniques, can serve as diagnostic tools to help instructors identify students in need of additional help, as well as providing students with a better awareness of their strengths and weaknesses and, correspondingly, ways to optimize their learning.

Given the obvious link between studying and learning (as established by high exam scores and course grades), a large self-help market caters to students looking for tips. The style and empirical basis of the available material vary greatly. Many of the guides include discussions of such topics as multiple intelligences, learning styles, and time management and provide step-by-step strategies on how to read better, take good notes, and remember and test better. Whereas some guides include some empirical evidence to support recommendations (e.g., Pauk & Owens, 2007; Tamblin & Ward, 2006), most do not. For example, Newport (2007) featured tips that were based on interviews with students who achieved high grades in college and listed anecdotes of what the high-scoring students did (e.g., minimize the time spent on assignments while still learning exactly what is needed; p. 83). Many guides target high school or first-year college students (Fry, 2004), and many of the prescriptions are not necessarily derived from or aligned with the empirical literature on study techniques reviewed previously.

Although there are many nonempirical self-help guides to studying that have been published in the past few years, there is a long history of research on study behaviors. Early attempts to assess study behaviors go back to Wrenn's (1933) Study-Habits Inventory, the Student Skills Inventory (Locke, 1940), and the Survey of Study Habits and Attitudes (SSHA; Brown & Holtzman, 1955). The SSHA comprises four major variables: delay avoidance, work methods, educational acceptance, and teacher approval. More recently, researchers have commonly used the Learning and Study Strategies Inventory (Weinstein & Palmer, 2002).

# WHAT IS BEST?

A large body of research has attempted to identify the optimal techniques for successful academic achievement and learning (e.g., Gurung, 2005; Hattie, Biggs, & Purdie, 1996; Kobayashi, 2006; Metcalfe, 2009; Robbins, Lauver, Le, Davis, & Langley, 2004; Wingate, 2006; Worrell et al., 2010; for extensive reviews and summaries, see Credé & Kuncel, 2008; Gurung & Schwartz, 2009; and Hattie, 2009). The extensive literature has been boiled down to two major domains: (a) heuristics that describe generic associations between pedagogy and learning and (b) findings about metacognition and self-regulated learning that illustrate how learners selectively apply and change their use of those heuristics (Winne & Nesbit, 2010). No clear strategies work all of the time, for all students, in all classes (e.g., Gurung, 2003; Hadwin & Winne, 1996; Hattie et al., 1996). Unfortunately, given the volume of past research and the ambiguity of findings (i.e., what is found to work in one study often does not seem to work in another), it is difficult for instructors to find the best empirically supported advice to give students regarding how to study.

Cognitive and educational psychology provide a short list of what the best ways to study may be (E. L. Bjork & Bjork, 2011; Matlin, 2002). For example, the unified learning model (ULM; Shell et al., 2010) suggests how motivational, cognitive, and neurobiological sciences can inform teaching and learning. The ULM stresses that new learning requires attention, effort, repetition, and making connections. The ULM also nicely reminds us that although "all neurons learn the same way" (p. 15), no instructional method or studying technique will lead to the same learning result for all students.

E. L. Bjork and Bjork (2011) pointed out that optimal learning may be best brought about by instructors creating a desirable level of difficulty. Desirable difficulties, that is, conditions of learning that require effort for the student and create difficulty, are said to actually lead to more durable and flexible learning (R. A. Bjork, 1994). The major suggestions for how to do this include

- varying conditions of practice (e.g., studying in different rooms),
- spacing study or practice sessions,
- interleaving versus blocking instruction (i.e., two sets of information are blended instead of presented in isolation) on separate to-be-learned tasks, and
- fostering generation of answers and self-tests.

Many empirical studies and robust data form the basis for each of these suggestions. For example, students studied Swahili vocabulary in one of four groups: One group studied and tested only those words they had not learned previously, another studied and tested all words, a third studied only words they felt unfamiliar with but were tested on all words, and the final group studied all words but were only tested on words they were unfamiliar with. The groups with repeated testing (i.e., tested on all words) showed the most recall (Karpicke & Roediger, 2008).

Students' impressions of what study behaviors are most helpful are not always accurate. Perlman, McCann, and Prust (2007) asked students what grade they would find acceptable in the course they were taking and also to rank the perceived effectiveness of different study behaviors. Using a 7-point grading scale (A, AB, B, BC, C, CD, F), 41% said they would be satisfied with a B and 31% a BC or lower. Only seven of 59 study behaviors were ranked as helping to "a great extent." From the most to least helpful, these seven study behaviors were as follows: attend class, do assignments on time, pay attention during class, take group work responsibilities seriously, study in a quiet setting, put extra effort into assignments worth more points, and do extra credit. All of these are certainly desirable, but most instructors would include other behaviors ranked much lower, such as read textbook/assignments before class (ranked 32), study 2 to 3 hours or more out of class for every hour in class (40), read the text/readings multiple times (51), review exams (56), use tutors (57), and so on. The authors found no significant relationship between final grades and students' beliefs about which behaviors helped earn those grades. Perlman and McCann (2002a) provided some insight regarding the behaviors that actually influence grades. They asked students whose scores from one exam to the next had increased or decreased one full letter grade how they had studied differently for the second of the two exams. The following behaviors were identified by more than 25% of those doing better on the second test: studied more hours, read book/text/readings more carefully, studied in a quiet environment with few interruptions, used study guide more, and read text/readings more times. Those doing worse identified the following behaviors: studied fewer hours, read book/text/readings less carefully, read text/readings fewer times, family or personal crisis interfered, missed more classes, and missing lecture notes.

In another study, the instructor surveyed students in Introductory Psychology regarding their use of 11 different study techniques. The three most frequently used study techniques were reading the text, reading notes, and using mnemonics (Gurung, 2005). Although these techniques were correlated with exam performance, they were not the strongest predictors of exam performance. Two less frequently used techniques, self-testing of knowledge and memorizing definitions, were the strongest predictors. In a similar study of 125 Introductory Psychology students' use of different study techniques, attendance, study guide use, using practice exams, and using class material to explain problems were positively correlated with exam scores (Gurung, Weidert, & Jeske, 2010).

Additional studies have provided some suggestions regarding how faculty can help students study better. These prescriptions can be naturally divided into what instructors can do themselves and what they can advise students to do.

## WHAT INSTRUCTORS CAN DO

### Prepare for Class

Although it is difficult for an instructor to have time before every class to review and prepare for that class meeting, consideration of how today's material is related to what came before and what comes after, as well as a number of other considerations (Perlman & McCann, 2008), can make the information more memorable and understandable. Prior course preparation allows the creation of well-organized lectures and presentations, and use of an outline format in the lecture notes allows easy presentation of the day's material on the board for ready reference in student creation of organized class notes. This outline and the lecture notes can be easily posted online for student reference, although the results of this practice are not always positive (Weatherly, Grabe, & Arthur, 2002–2003). There is some evidence that providing handouts of lecture slide shows (Gier & Kreiner, 2009) is beneficial to students, but see Noppe (2007) for an exception. How much is provided makes a difference. Providing a skeletal or partial outline improved student test performance more than additional detailed handouts (Cornelius & Owen-DeSchryver, 2008; Russell, Caris, Harris, & Hendricson, 1983). Giving students unlimited access to notes has also been linked to higher grades (Hove & Corcoran, 2008). In general, allowing access to some material, preferably outlines, seems to help students learn.

### Make Classes Interesting and Important Points Memorable

"Unfortunately, as teachers, we often spend less time cultivating an audience than we do preparing for that audience" (Sleigh & Ritzer, 2004, p. 287). The first step toward bringing an instructor's outstanding classroom material to the attention of the students is to get them to show up for the class. As one might expect, attendance influences course grades (Buckalew, Daly, & Coffield, 1986; Gurung, 2005). One of the most important factors influencing attendance is the amount of material from the classroom that appears on the test (Sleigh, Ritzer, & Casey, 2002), so one way to get students to come is to include material not available in the book or from other assignments in class presentations and to include questions on that material in the test. Another is to use periodic quizzes, especially on topics discussed in class. Mixing lecture with videos and discussions (see Kramer & Korn, 1999, for suggestions on managing discussions) and creating a more engaged classroom environment, including use of asking students questions, encourage attendance and attention. Although asking students questions in class can lead to uncomfortable periods of silence, Larkin and Pines (2008) provided a number of suggestions to make participation more likely, including creating an environment conducive to participation, establishing a norm of participation, starting with safe questions (a show of hands) to break the ice, asking students to write down answers before seeking a verbal response, and practicing active listening techniques.

Providing good content and being interesting and/or entertaining should not be seen as mutually exclusive. The use of good examples and humor makes class more interesting and attendance more likely. Vivid and memorable examples help form connections to existing knowledge, actively organize understanding, and add to content knowledge of the subject (Galliano, 1999). Students often report better memory of humorous examples; Powers (2008, p. 61) suggested making the humor relevant; using entertaining clips from movies, TV, or popular songs; using oneself as a humorous example; and stockpiling humorous stories from students and humorous exam questions.

### Prepare Students for Exams

Psychologists have discovered many useful learning principles that can be used to improve the acquisition and retention of information. Unfortunately, some of the following tried-and-true ideas may not be used by students as they study:

- *The spacing (distributed study) effect.* "It is consistently found that when practice trials are spaced far apart (distributed practice), performance is superior to what it is when practice trials are close together (massed practice)" (Olson & Hergenhahn, 2009, p. 132; see also Pyc & Dunlosky, 2010). Students should be encouraged to study throughout the semester and not just cram on the eve of the exam.
- *Aristotle's law of frequency.* In the study of learning, frequency is often equated with repetition, so the more "trials" one experiences, the better the learning of that material should be. This suggests that students should read the book more than once, go over their notes frequently, and study other material several times prior to an exam.

- *Ebbinghaus's overlearning effect.* Learning or continuing to practice beyond mastery (overlearning) "reduces the rate of forgetting considerably" (Olson & Hergenhahn, 2009, p. 41). Students often go over material until they "recognize" it on review, but do not really "know" it. They need to continue to study the material beyond this point, ask themselves questions about it, apply it to their lives, and so on, until they really have it mastered.

Unfortunately, many students still cram the night before the test, stop studying when they think they have an adequate grasp of the material, read the book only once before the test, or use pedagogical aids poorly (Gurung, 2003, 2004). Instructors could easily remind students of the previous principles prior to an exam and offer examples of the advantages that these approaches would provide.

Instructors can try to improve the chances that students will study the proper material by providing study guides prior to exams, indicating the most important concepts or material to concentrate on (Dickson, Miller, & Devoley, 2005; Flora & Logan, 1996). A number of resources provide empirically validated ways to develop study guides (Conderman & Bresnahan, 2010; Khogali, Laidlaw, & Harden, 2006). On the other hand, this may limit the material students study and may not be appropriate if the instructor wants them to study all of the material assigned and topics discussed in class. Holding test review sessions can also help students understand difficult concepts; identify areas where more study is needed; and, if done well, promote student motivation and engagement (Gurung & Bord, 2008). Students who attend review sessions do better on the test compared with those who do not attend, an effect only partially accounted for by student GPA (i.e., smarter students attending the review sessions). Another positive step is the preparation and provision of a rubric describing how an essay exam will be scored and, for use after the exam, identifying the types of responses that will be scored as correct answers. Instructors also should provide opportunities for looking over a test after it has been given, so students can see the errors they made and, possibly, improve their performance on the next test. Ambrose, Bridges, DiPietro, Lovett, and Norman (2010) recommended using "exam wrappers," short handouts that students complete when an exam is handed back to them that help them analyze their own performance (p. 251).

Another consideration involves meeting the needs of students with disabilities or other problems. Instructors should familiarize themselves with the services and policies of their institution and make certain that course material meets accessibility requirements and that both instructor and student understand the expectations of the other (Boyd, 2008). Dealing with students with other types of problems can be another source of concern for instructors, and different considerations may be required to properly handle individual cases (Perlman, McCann, & Kadah-Ammeter, 2008).

## WHAT STUDENTS CAN DO

Students should take responsibility for their own learning. Approximately 55% of the variance in learning is accounted for by student factors (Hattie, 2009). "The fact that students in the end must do their own learning (and that some will fail) is a universal truth" (Perlman, McCann, & McFadden, 2008, p. 344). The literature on student learning has provided the following suggestions for students to improve studying and learning. Suggestions with a strong empirical basis are shown with a citation. Those suggestions provided by cognitive and educational psychology theorizing but without explicit empirical testing appear sans citation and are fertile ground for future research.

- Get enough sleep. Behavioral studies of humans and other species find that sleep plays a critical role in posttraining memory consolidation (Walker & Stickgold, 2004). It is not surprising that if the student is half asleep in class or while studying, attention, learning, and performance will suffer. In particular, the common practice of pulling an all-nighter before an exam is less likely to produce positive results than distributed studying leading up to a good night's sleep before the test, although it is probably better than no studying at all.

- Have frequent short study sessions, rather than infrequent long study sessions. Landrum, Turrisi, and Brandel (2006) reported that A and B students tended to increase studying frequency as the semester progressed but to decrease the time spent on each study event. They studied more often, but each study session was shorter than the lower scoring students.

- Avoid study practices that do not work well (Gurung, 2005, p. 241; Gurung et al., 2010). These practices include spending too much time on key terms or summaries and not enough on other areas such as review questions; highlighting too much text and thus obscuring the important points; studying chapter review questions rather than using them to test knowledge; and studying with TV or music, surfing the net while studying, and nonproductive studying with others (Gurung, 2005; Gurung et al., 2010).

- Buy or have other access to the textbook (read book/text/readings more carefully; Perlman & McCann, 2002b).
- Read the class syllabus carefully.
- Attend classes (Buckalew, Daly, & Coffield, 1986; Sleigh & Ritzer, 2004). Sit toward the front of the room (Benedict & Hoag, 2004); take advantage of note-taking instruction/guides (Robin et al., 1977); and take good notes and then review, organize, and clarify them (missing lecture notes; Perlman & McCann, 2002a).
- Schedule regular times during the day to study and complete homework, and spend enough time to do a good job (good time management; Loomis, 2000).
- Delay other pleasurable activities until studying is completed. Study more hours (Perlman & McCann, 2002a, 2002b), but make sure the studying is without distractions and deliberate (Plant, Ericsson, Hill, & Asberg, 2005).
- Organize your study activities (Dickinson & O'Connell, 1990); for example, make lists of things to accomplish while studying, identify the steps needed to complete the task, and keep a study log listing things you have done and need to do.
- Review material prior to reading it, and write out the general outline of major points and subheadings that organize the chapter (usually readily apparent in bold or colored print).
- Read the book or other assigned material prior to coming to class (see Boyd, 2004, for suggestions), and pay attention to make sure you understand what you are reading.
- Read the assigned material more than once (law of frequency; see Olson & Hergenhahn, 2009).
- Use the study guide (Gurung et al., 2010; Perlman & McCann, 2002a).
- Memorize important material through repetition when necessary, and once you feel you have it mastered, study it a little more (overlearning; see Olson & Hergenhahn, 2009) to help improve mastery and retention.
- Create applied examples and mnemonics to help remember points (Gurung, 2005).
- Use a study partner (ideally someone doing at least as well as you in the class); try to explain the material to each other, and test yourselves on your knowledge.
- Use chapter review questions and other material to test your knowledge (Gurung, 2005).
- Review assignments before going to class.

- Review exams, with special attention to items missed or guessed at.
- If you are not doing well, try to get a tutor.
- Create an outline before beginning to write a paper, rewrite the initial drafts, and start working on the paper as early as possible (Hattie, 2009).
- Check your work before handing in assignments (Hattie, 2009).

## FUTURE RESEARCH

Although we continue to learn more about which approaches to studying work and which do not, there is much we either do not know or know in insufficient detail. One area ripe for future scholarship of teaching and learning (SoTL) is the use of the Internet and other technologies as study tools. To experience what some call "true learning," a student needs to participate in an interactive learning environment (Katz-Navon, Naveh, & Stern, 2009). The way students have learned has been correlated with new emerging technological advances in society and changing demographics (Black, 2010). Students today rely heavily on technology. They get most of their information from Internet sources that tend to be faster than other means (Black, 2010). Many of the suggestions from cognitive psychology for studying, such as those discussed previously, can be made possible using online study aids that accompany textbooks, although the research in this area is still in its infancy. Students who regularly access online homework sites show improvements in grades on exams and quizzes (Biktimirov & Klassen, 2008). Online learning aids such as Connect, Learnsmart, MyEconLab, Aplia, and WebWork have also been shown to be effective tools to enhance a student's overall engagement and grades (Burch & Kuo, 2010; Nguyen & Trimarchi, 2010; Smolira, 2008). These programs directly use cognitive psychology best practices. For example, Learnsmart, a McGraw-Hill product, allows students to be connected to a study tool from an iPod, computer, iPhone, or any Internet capable technology. Study material is provided on the basis of the student's weak and strong areas by adjusting to the user's performance. This program allows students to save time on studying by providing tools to fit the needs of every type of learner. In a classroom test (Introductory Psychology), the correlation between student exam scores and Learnsmart use, after controlling for student GPA, was .29 (Gurung, 2011). Much more research of this type is called for to test the efficacy of online study aids.

Another area ripe for future SoTL is the generalizability of laboratory studies to actual classrooms. One of the main hindrances to the generation of empirically based suggestions for studying is that there is not yet enough translational research testing the results of the lab studies in the classroom.

For example, a lab study with college students showed the effectiveness of the 3R (read-recite-review) strategy for learning from texts (McDaniel, Howard, & Einstein, 2009), but will the same finding be true for a student studying for a class? We need to test the methods we espouse in students' usual study environments and where there is something at stake—it is one thing for students to memorize and recall words in a lab for extra credit and a completely different matter when students are studying for an exam with both an exam grade and a course grade at stake. This contextual testing will ensure that more of the proximal psychological processes are taken into account and will also require more longitudinal studies of learning in the classroom compared with one-time, postintervention measurements (Winne & Nesbit, 2010, p. 655). Recommendations for studying that emerge from cognitive research on core principles of learning conducted in the lab may not always work in the context of students learning classroom material for an exam (Daniel & Poole, 2009).

## CONCLUSION

Exhibit 6.1 summarizes key recommendations for faculty, and Exhibit 6.2 summarizes key areas for future SoTL research on this topic. Many of the recommendations in this chapter, although empirically tested in classrooms, may not work in all classrooms. For example, making lecture outlines available before class may lead to lower attendance. Like a good replication, the hallmark of science, we need to always monitor how our students are studying and which efforts pay off. The reality is that learning is influenced by a variety of factors, and both instructors and students play roles.

### EXHIBIT 6.1
Evidence-Based Recommendations for Teachers

- Use an outline format to prepare for class lectures, and make the outline available to students, when appropriate.
- Encourage attendance by using humor in lectures, using in-class quizzes, and including questions on lecture content on exams.
- Tie concepts to real life with good examples, and ask students for examples (which can be retained for use in later semesters).
- Hold review sessions prior to exams, and consider providing study guides indicating the most important points and concepts to be studied.
- If a student is not doing well, ask about his or her attendance, study habits, and behaviors; point out practices that are unlikely to be helpful; and suggest better approaches.
- Stress the importance of a healthy life style, especially getting adequate sleep.

## EXHIBIT 6.2
## Questions for Future Research

- Does increasing student metacognition lead to changes in study behavior following the intervention?
- Do students modify their study behaviors after receiving a bad grade on an exam?
- How can instructors improve student study skills?
- How do lab-based findings translate into the classroom?
- Is training students to use the 3R studying method (McDaniel et al., 2009) effective in the class?
- Do exam wrappers (Ambrose et al., 2010) change students' studying behavior?
- Does online diagnostic quizzing increase student learning?
- Does using Connect, MyPsychLab, or PsychPortal increase student learning?
- Do students who practice healthy lifestyles learn better, and will improvements in health over a semester improve studying and learning?
- How can social networking sites (e.g., Facebook) be used in the classroom to facilitate communication between students and between student and instructor, and consequently to improve learning?
- What are the best ways to use personal devices such as smart phones for learning?
- How does the online delivery of material (e.g., digital textbooks) change how students read and study?

# REFERENCES

Ambrose, S. A., Bridges, M. W., DiPietro, M., Lovett, M. C., & Norman, M. K. (2010). *How learning works: 7 research-based principles for smart teaching.* San Francisco, CA: Jossey-Bass.

Benedict, M. E., & Hoag, J. (2004). Seating location in large lectures: Are seating preferences or location related to course performance? *The Journal of Economic Education, 35,* 215–231. doi:10.3200/JECE.35.3.215-231

Biktimirov, E. N., & Klassen, K. J. (2008). Relationship between use of online support materials and student performance in an introductory finance course. *Journal of Education for Business, 83,* 153–158. doi:10.3200/JOEB.83.3.153-158

Bjork, E. L., & Bjork, R. (2011). Making things harder on yourself, but in a good way: Creating desirable difficulties to enhance learning. In M. A., Gernsbacher, R. W. Pew, L. M. Hough, & J. R. Pomerantz (Eds.), *Psychology and the real world: Essays illustration fundamental contributions to society* (pp. 56–64). New York, NY: Worth.

Bjork, R. A. (1994). Memory and metamemory considerations in the training of human beings. In J. Metcalfe and A. Shimamura (Eds.), *Metacognition: Knowing about knowing* (pp. 185–205). Cambridge, MA: MIT Press.

Black, A. (2010). Gen Y: Who they are and how they learn. *Educational Horizons, 88,* 92–101.

Boyd, D. R. (2004). Using textbooks effectively: Getting students to read them. In B. Perlman, L. I. McCann, & S. H. McFadden (Eds.), *Lessons learned: Practical advice for the teaching of psychology* (Vol. 2, pp. 295–302). Washington, DC: Association for Psychological Science.

Boyd, D. R. (2008). Teaching students with disabilities: A proactive approach. In B. Perlman, L. I. McCann, & S. H. McFadden (Eds.), *Lessons learned: Practical advice for the teaching of psychology* (Vol. 3, pp. 99–108). Washington, DC: Association for Psychological Science.

Brown, W. F., & Holtzman, W. H. (1955). A study-attitudes questionnaire for predicting academic success. *Journal of Educational Psychology, 46,* 75–84. doi:10.1037/h0039970

Buckalew, L. W., Daly, J. D., & Coffield, K. E. (1986). Relationship of initial class attendance and seating location to academic performance in psychology classes. *Bulletin of the Psychonomic Society, 24,* 63–64.

Burch, K. J., & Kuo, Y. (2010). Traditional vs. online homework in college algebra. *Mathematics and Computer Education, 44,* 53–63.

Conderman, G., & Bresnahan, V. (2010). Study guides to the rescue. *Intervention in School and Clinic, 45*(3), 169–176. doi:10.1177/1053451209349532

Cornelius, T. L., & Owen-DeSchryver, J. (2008). Differential effects of full and partial notes on learning outcomes and attendance. *Teaching of Psychology, 35,* 6–12. doi:10.1080/00986280701818466

Credé, M., & Kuncel, N. R. (2008). Study habits, skills, and attitudes: The third pillar supporting collegiate academic performance. *Perspectives on Psychological Science, 3,* 425–453. doi:10.1111/j.1745-6924.2008.00089.x

Daniel, D. B., & Poole, D. A. (2009). Learning for life: An ecological approach to pedagogical research. *Perspectives on Psychological Science, 4,* 91–96. doi:10.1111/j.1745-6924.2009.01095.x

Dickinson, D. J., & O'Connell, D. Q. (1990). Effect of quality and quantity of study on student grades. *Journal of Educational Research, 83,* 227–231.

Dickson, L. K., Miller, M. D., & Devoley, M. S. (2005). Effect of textbook study guides on student performance in introductory psychology. *Teaching of Psychology, 32,* 34–39. doi:10.1207/s15328023top3201_8

Dunlosky, J., & Graesser, A. C. (Eds.). (2009). *Metacognition in educational theory and practice.* Mahwah, NJ: Erlbaum.

Entwistle, N. (2009). *Teaching for understanding at university: Deep approaches and distinctive ways of thinking.* London, England: Palgrave Macmillan.

Flora, S. R., & Logan, R. E. (1996). Using computerized study guides to increase performance on general psychology examinations: An experimental analysis. *Psychological Reports, 79,* 235–241. doi:10.2466/pr0.1996.79.1.235

Fry, R. (2004). *How to study* (6th ed.). Clifton Park, NY: Thompson Delmar Learning.

Galliano, G. (1999). Enhancing student learning through exemplary examples. In B. Perlman, L. I. McCann, & S. H. McFadden (Eds.), *Lessons learned: Practical advice for the teaching of psychology* (Vol. 1, pp. 87–92). Washington, DC: Association for Psychological Science.

Gettinger, M., & Seibert, J. K. (2002). Contributions of study skills to academic competence. *School Psychology Review*, *31*, 350–365.

Gier, V., & Kreiner, D. (2009). Incorporating active learning with PowerPoint-based lectures using content-based questions. *Teaching of Psychology*, *36*, 134–139. doi:10.1080/00986280902739792

Gurung, R. A. R. (2003). Pedagogical aids and student performance. *Teaching of Psychology*, *30*, 92–95. doi:10.1207/S15328023TOP3002_01

Gurung, R. A. R. (2004). Pedagogical aids: Learning enhancers or dangerous detours? *Teaching of Psychology*, *31*, 164–166. doi:10.1207/s15328023top3103_1

Gurung, R. A. R. (2005). How do students really study (and does it matter)? *Teaching of Psychology*, *32*, 239–241.

Gurung, R. A. R. (2011, June). *If they study, they will learn: What teachers need to know and do to make this so.* Opening keynote address at Eastern Teachers of Psychology Conference, Staunton, VA.

Gurung, R. A. R., & Bord, D. (2008). Enhancing learning and exam preparation: The review session. In B. Perlman, L. I. McCann, & S. H. McFadden (Eds.), *Lessons learned: Practical advice for the teaching of psychology* (Vol. 3, pp. 131–138). Washington, DC: Association for Psychological Science.

Gurung, R. A. R., & Schwartz, B. M. (2009). *Optimizing teaching and learning: Pedagogical research in practice.* Malden, MA: Blackwell.

Gurung, R. A. R., Weidert, J., & Jeske, A. S. (2010). A closer look at how students study (and if it matters). *Journal of the Scholarship of Teaching and Learning*, *10*, 28–33.

Gurung, R. A. R., & Wilson-Doenges, G. (2010). Engaging students in psychology: Building on first-year programs and seminars. In D. S. Dunn, B. C. Beins, M. A. McCarthy, & G. W. Hill (Eds.), *Best practices for beginnings and endings in the psychology major* (pp. 93–106). New York, NY: Oxford University Press.

Hacker, D., Dunlosky, J., & Graesser, A. (2009). *Handbook of metacognition in education.* New York, NY: Routledge/Taylor & Francis Group.

Hadwin, A. F., & Winne, P. H. (1996). Study strategies have meager support: A review with recommendations for implementation. *Journal of Higher Education*, *67*, 692–715. doi:10.2307/2943817

Hattie, J. (2009). *Visible learning: A synthesis of over 800 meta-analyses relating to achievement.* London, England: Routledge.

Hattie, J., Biggs, J., & Purdie, N. (1996). Effect of learning skills interventions on student learning: A meta-analysis. *Review of Educational Research*, *66*, 99–136.

Hove, M., & Corcoran, K. (2008). If you post it, will they come? Lecture availability in introductory psychology. *Teaching of Psychology*, *35*, 91–95. doi:10.1080/00986280802004560

Karpicke, J. D., & Roediger, H. L. (2008). The critical importance of retrieval for learning. *Science*, *319*, 966–968. doi:10.1126/science.1152408

Katz-Navon, T., Naveh, E., & Stern, Z. (2009). Active learning: When is more better? The case of resident physicians' medical errors. *Journal of Applied Psychology*, *94*, 1200–1209. doi:10.1037/a0015979

Khogali, S. E., Laidlaw, J., & Harden, R. (2006). Study guides: A study of different formats. *Medical Teacher*, 28, 375–377. doi:10.1080/01421590600799059

Kobayashi, K. (2006). Combined effects of note-taking/reviewing on learning and the enhancement through interventions: A meta-analytic review. *Educational Psychology*, 26, 459–477. doi:10.1080/01443410500342070

Kramer, T. J., & Korn, J. H. (1999). Class discussions: Promoting participation and preventing problems. In B. Perlman, L. I. McCann, & S. H. McFadden (Eds.), *Lessons learned: Practical advice for the teaching of psychology* (Vol. 1, pp. 99–104). Washington, DC: Association for Psychological Science.

Landrum, R. E., Turrisi, R., & Brandel, J. M. (2006). College students' study time, course level, time of semester, and grade earned. *Psychological Reports*, 98, 675–682. doi:10.2466/pr0.98.3.675-682

Larkin, J. E., & Pines, H. A. (2008). Asking questions: Promoting student-faculty interchange in the classroom. In B. Perlman, L. I. McCann, & S. H. McFadden (Eds.), *Lessons learned: Practical advice for the teaching of psychology* (Vol. 3, pp. 41–51). Washington, DC: Association for Psychological Science.

Locke, N. M. (1940). The Student Skills Inventory: A study habits test. *Journal of Applied Psychology*, 24, 493–504. doi:10.1037/h0058668

Loomis, K. D. (2000). Learning styles and asynchronous learning: Comparing the LASSI model to class performance. *Journal of Asynchronous Learning Networks*, 4, 23–32.

Marton, F., & Saljnoppeo, R. (1976). On quantitative differences in learning: I—Outcomes and process. *British Journal of Educational Psychology*, 46, 4–11. doi:10.1111/j.2044-8279.1976.tb02980.x

Matlin, M. W. (2002). Cognitive psychology and college-level pedagogy: Two siblings that rarely communicate. In D. F. Halpern & M. D. Hakel (Eds.), *Applying the science of leaning to university and beyond* (87–103). San Francisco, CA: Jossey-Bass.

McDaniel, M., Howard, D., & Einstein, G. (2009). The read-recite-review study strategy: Effective and portable. *Psychological Science*, 20, 516–522. doi:10.1111/j.1467-9280.2009.02325.x

Metcalfe, J. (2009). Metacognitive judgments and control of study. *Current Directions in Psychological Science*, 18, 159–163. doi:10.1111/j.1467-8721.2009.01628.x

Newport, C. (2007). *How to become a straight-A student: The unconventional strategies real college students use to score high while studying less.* New York, NY: Broadway Books.

Nguyen, T., & Trimarchi, A. (2010). Active learning in introductory economics: Do MyEconLab and Aplia make any difference? *International Journal for the Scholarship of Teaching and Learning*, 4, 1–18.

Noppe, I. (2007). PowerPoint presentation handouts and college student learning outcomes. *International Journal for the Scholarship of Teaching and Learning*, 1(1). Retrieved from http://www.georgiasouthern.edu/ijsotl

Olson, M. H., & Hergenhahn, B. R. (2009). *An introduction to theories of learning* (8th ed.). Upper Saddle River: NJ: Pearson Prentice Hall.

Pauk, W., & Owens, R. J. Q. (2007). *How to study in college* (9th ed.). San Francisco, CA: Wadsworth.

Perlman, B., & McCann, L. I. (2002a). Student perspectives on grade changes from test to test. *Teaching of Psychology, 29,* 51–53.

Perlman, B., & McCann, L. I. (2002b). What we need to know about teaching and teachers. In B. W. Buskist & V. Hevern (Eds.), *Essays from e-xcellence in teaching, 2000-2001.* Available at http://teachpsych.org/ebooks/eit2000/index.php

Perlman, B., & McCann, L. I. (2008). Preparing for a class session. In B. Perlman, L. I. McCann, & S. H. McFadden (Eds.), *Lessons learned: Practical advice for the teaching of psychology* (Vol. 3, pp. 15–22). Washington, DC: Association for Psychological Science.

Perlman, B., McCann, L. I., & Kadah-Ammeter, T. L. (2008). Working with students in need: An ethical perspective. In B. Perlman, L. I. McCann, & S. H. McFadden (Eds.), *Lessons learned: Practical advice for the teaching of psychology* (Vol. 3, pp. 325–334). Washington, DC: Association for Psychological Science.

Perlman, B., McCann, L. I., & McFadden, S. H. (2008). Observations on teaching: Fifteen years of teaching tips. In B. Perlman, L. I. McCann, & S. H. McFadden (Eds.), *Lessons learned: Practical advice for the teaching of psychology* (Vol. 3, pp. 337–346). Washington, DC: Association for Psychological Science.

Perlman, B., McCann, L. I., & Prust, A. (2007). Students' grades and ratings of perceived effectiveness of behaviors influencing academic performance. *Teaching of Psychology, 34,* 236–240. doi:10.1080/00986280701700284

Plant, E., Ericsson, K., Hill, L., & Asberg, K. (2005). Why study time does not predict grade point average across college students: Implications of deliberate practice for academic performance. *Contemporary Educational Psychology, 30,* 96–116. doi:10.1016/j.cedpsych.2004.06.001

Powers, T. (2008). Engaging students with humor. In B. Perlman, L. I. McCann, & S. H. McFadden (Eds.), *Lessons learned: Practical advice for the teaching of psychology* (Vol. 3, pp. 53–62). Washington, DC: Association for Psychological Science.

Prevatt, F., Petscher, Y., Proctor, B. E., Hurst, A., & Adams, K. (2006). The revised Learning and Study Strategies Inventory: An evaluation of competing models. *Educational and Psychological Measurement, 66,* 448–458. doi:10.1177/0013164405282454

Pyc, M. A., & Dunlosky, J. (2010). Toward an understanding of students' allocation of study time: Why do they decide to mass or space their practice? *Memory & Cognition, 38,* 431–440. doi:10.3758/MC.38.4.431

Robbins, S. B., Lauver, K., Le, H., Davis, D., & Langley, R. (2004). Do psychological and study skill factors predict college outcomes? A meta-analysis. *Psychological Bulletin, 130,* 261–288. doi:10.1037/0033-2909.130.2.261

Robin, A., Foxx, R. M., Martello, J., & Archable, C. (1977). Teaching note-taking skills to underachieving college students. *The Journal of Educational Research, 71,* 81–85.

Russell, I. J., Caris, T. N., Harris, G. D., & Hendricson, W. D. (1983). Effects of three types of lecture notes on medical student achievement. *Journal of Medical Education*, 58, 627–636.

Shell, D. F., Brooks, D. W., Trainin, G., Wilson, K. M., Kauffman, D. F., & Herr, L. M. (2010). *The Unified Learning Model: How motivational, cognitive, and neurobiological sciences inform best teaching practices*. New York, NY: Springer.

Sleigh, M. J., & Ritzer, D. R. (2004). Encouraging student attendance. In B. Perlman, L. I. McCann, & S. H. McFadden (Eds.), *Lessons learned: Practical advice for the teaching of psychology* (Vol. 2, pp. 287–293). Washington, DC: Association for Psychological Science.

Sleigh, M. J., Ritzer, D. R., & Casey, M. B. (2002). Student versus faculty perceptions of missing class. *Teaching of Psychology*, 29, 53–56.

Smolira, J. C. (2008). Student perceptions of online homework in introductory finance courses. *Journal of Education for Business*, 84, 90–95. doi:10.3200/JOEB.84.2.90-95

Tamblin, L., & Ward, P. (2006). *The smart study guide: Psychological techniques for student success*. Malden, MA: Blackwell.

Walker, M. P., & Stickgold, R. (2004). Sleep dependent learning and memory consolidation. *Neuron*, 44, 121–133. doi:10.1016/j.neuron.2004.08.031

Weatherly, J. N., Grabe, M., & Arthur, E. I. L. (2002-2003). Providing introductory psychology students access to lecture slides, via Blackboard 5: A negative impact on performance. *Journal of Educational Technology Systems*, 31, 463–474. doi:10.2190/KRW7-QHFY-AY3M-FFJC

Weinstein, C. E., & Palmer, D. R. (2002). *Learning and Study Strategies Inventory (LASSI): User's manual* (2nd ed.). Clearwater, FL: H & H Publishing.

Wingate, U. (2006). Doing away with "study skills." *Teaching in Higher Education*, 11, 457–469. doi:10.1080/13562510600874268

Winne, P. H., & Nesbit, J. C. (2010). The psychology of academic achievement. *Annual Review of Psychology*, 61, 653–678. doi:10.1146/annurev.psych.093008.100348

Worrell, F. C., Casad, B. J., Daniel, D. B., McDaniel, M., Messer, W. S., Miller, H. L.,... Zlokovich, M. S. (2010). Promising principles for translating psychological science into teaching and learning. In D. F. Halpern (Ed.), *Undergraduate education in psychology: A blueprint for the future of the discipline* (129–144). Washington, DC: American Psychological Association. doi:10.1037/12063-008

Wrenn, C. G. (1933). *Study-habits inventory*. Oxford, England: Stanford University Press.

# 7

## SELECTION OF TEXTBOOKS
## OR READINGS FOR YOUR COURSE

R. ERIC LANDRUM

In the design and implementation of teaching for a college course, it is important to consider which textbook or readings to use. Course design experts (Fink, 2003; Wiggins & McTighe, 1998) emphasize that the textbook should not drive the course but should instead be used to achieve course goals. But what factors influence a text's compatibility with course goals? One cannot assume that newer texts necessarily reflect cognitive learning principles. Indeed, there is little published evidence that fundamental cognitive psychology principles are routinely embedded as part of textbook design (Matlin, 2002; but see Winne & Nesbit, 2010, for a recent review). Rather, changes in textbooks tend to reflect developments in the subject field. For example, Weiten and Wight (1992) provided an overview of the history of publishing introductory psychology textbooks, suggesting that content changes in textbooks are due to (a) research progress in psychology, (b) new pedagogical techniques and changing student demographics, (c) societal and cultural change, and (d) publishing industry influences.

In this chapter, I first summarize general advice from other authors about textbook selection. Next, I summarize the research on factors affecting textbook selection. Finally, I discuss the possibility of using course readings.

## GENERAL ADVICE FROM OTHER AUTHORS
## ABOUT TEXTBOOK SELECTION

In compendia offering broad teaching advice, the topic of textbook selection is frequently mentioned (Christopher, 2006; Davis, 1993; Lucas & Bernstein, 2005; McKeachie, 2002; Robinson, 1994). McKeachie (2002) suggested a procedure in which students choose a single textbook for the course from a short list of two or three textbooks or suggest that different books be made available at the bookstore for the same course. Such involvement might encourage students to feel empowered and share ownership in the textbook selection process. Although databases do exist that systematically review difficulty level, length, chapter topics and organization, pedagogical aids, and core vocabulary variables of introductory psychology textbooks (e.g., Griggs, 2006), there is not much advice offered to psychology instructors as to how to apply these criteria in the actual evaluation and selection of textbooks.

Textbook selection is a topic not limited to psychology instruction, and advice about textbook selection practices is available from other disciplines. Dowie (1981) and Hartley and Ross (1985) provided structured checklists that organize singular evaluative items into familiar rubrics (e.g., range of subject, pedagogical features). Bartlett and Morgan (1991) developed a specialized checklist designed to help instructors of multiple sections of the same course make textbook decisions. Insightful advice about textbook publishing is available from authors of psychology textbooks (Matlin, 1997; Matthews & Davis, 1999; Myers, 2007).

## RESEARCH ABOUT TEXTBOOK SELECTION VARIABLES

The ubiquitous textbook is a topic of interest to researchers in many fields. As I reviewed this broad literature, four themes emerged: research about (a) physical textbook features (e.g., page length), (b) objective measures (e.g., frequency counts of books published in a content area), (c) content analyses of textbooks based on core terms, and (d) content analyses based on other elements (e.g., pedagogical aids). Each of these areas is briefly reviewed here.

### Physical Characteristics

Studies that examine the physical (i.e., static, fixed) characteristics of textbooks can be divided into three types: (a) comparison studies that address only objective features; (b) content analysis studies that examine and identify the core terms within a specialty area; and (c) content analysis studies that are based on content other than core terms, such as main ideas or major theories. If an instructor wanted to base his or her textbook selection in part on objective criteria, the resources provided by the following types of studies can be invaluable.

## Objective Features

There are at least two different approaches to the examination of objective features. A discipline-wide approach could be used to examine the sheer number of textbooks available or the number of new books per year published in specialty areas within a discipline (Chatman & Goetz, 1985). The benefit of this approach is that trends can be tracked over time. Most research in this genre is limited to a subspecialty or a particular course within a discipline. For example, Christopher, Griggs, and Hagans (2000) completed an analysis of the physical characteristics of 14 social psychology textbooks and 17 abnormal psychology textbooks; Marek and Griggs (2001) completed a similar physical characteristics analysis for 17 cognitive psychology textbooks.

Numerous sources are available that summarize the characteristics of the introductory psychology textbook (Griggs, Jackson, Christopher, & Marek, 1999; Griggs, Jackson, & Napolitano, 1994; Griggs & Koenig, 2001). Others have used physical characteristics for objective analysis but subsequently included student or faculty attitude/opinion surveys—those studies are presented later. Examination of physical characteristics alone yields helpful information when selecting a textbook, such as the feature set of the textbook. Another approach within the domain of objective features analysis involves the identification of core concepts.

## Content Analyses Based on Core Terms

A recurring theme in the teaching of psychology literature has been the content analysis of core items from introductory psychology textbooks (Griggs, Bujak-Johnson, & Proctor, 2004; Landrum, 1993; Quereshi, 1993; Zechmeister & Zechmeister, 2000). With regard to a core terminology to use for textbook selection, the outcomes may be troubling. Depending on the methodology used in the previously cited core content studies, the core number of items in introductory psychology textbooks ranges from three concepts to 126 concepts.

Zechmeister and Zechmeister (2000) reported that "the lack of convergent validity is obvious and troubling" (p. 9), or with perhaps a more positive interpretation, "the results of our studies and those of others suggest that if psychology has a common language, there are many dialects" (p. 10). In some respects, the lack of a common core in introductory psychology may also reflect the fragmentation believed to exist in psychology today (Dunn et al., 2010).

## Content Analyses Based on Content Other Than Core Terms

Microlevel content analysis approaches are characterized as examining variables at the elemental level, such as objective tallies of the occurrence of features (e.g., pedagogical aids) or the occurrence of basic ideas (e.g., core terms). Some researchers have taken a more macrolevel approach as a method of textbook comparison and selection. For instance, Griggs and Marek (2001) and Griggs, Jackson, Marek, and Christopher (1998) compared introductory psychology textbooks by examining critical-thinking sections and the citations used. Goldstein, Siegel, and Seaman (2009) reviewed how disability-related topics were presented in 24 introductory psychology textbooks. Other types of content analyses used to compare textbooks have included an analysis of the most frequently cited books (Griggs, Proctor, & Cook, 2004), of the most frequently cited journal articles and authors (Gorenflo & McConnell, 1991), and of scientific thinking and statistical thinking sections of textbooks (Griggs et al., 1998). As an instructor, if you wish to focus on a particular aspect of the typical textbook—such as a book that focuses on critical thinking—a macrolevel approach as described here could be useful.

## INSTRUCTOR AND STUDENT VARIABLES

Logically, the participants in formal research studies about textbooks have been faculty members and students. Research with faculty members centers on measuring their opinions about textbooks, and student-based research expands beyond opinions only to include studies about student use of textbooks and how textbooks may influence course performance. Both of these research areas are briefly reviewed here.

## Research Based on Faculty Opinion

Research that is based on faculty opinion falls into two categories: (a) journal article authors completing an analysis of textbooks, and (b) journal article authors surveying other faculty members and then analyzing quantitative data. In psychology, these types of studies have been published by Altman, Ericksen, and Pena-Shaff (2006); Landrum and Hormel (2002); Weiten (1988); and Yonker, Cummins-Sebree, Marshall, and Zai (2007). The approaches used tend to mirror the approach used in the analysis of the physical characteristics of a textbook. That is, some researchers examine broad content-based categories such as theories, theoretical approaches, and discipline-based orientations, and other researchers focus on the importance of certain textbook features. In an analysis of selection criteria regarding psychology textbooks, Landrum and Hormel (2002) reported that the top five criteria for faculty (with 1 = *most important*) were as follows: (a) accuracy, (b) readability/writing quality, (c) examples, (d) currency of research, and (e) research base; they also found that the faculty textbook selection criteria do not map perfectly onto the faculty perceptions of what helps students learn responses. For example, faculty members highly rated "currency of research" as important for textbook selection, but moderately rated "currency of research" for importance to student learning. Additionally, for some dimensions, instructor experience influences selection criteria. For instance, more experienced instructors place more importance on diagrams and figures, and less experienced instructors place more importance on the availability of ancillary materials that accompany the textbook.

## Research Based on Student Opinion, Use, and Performance Outcomes

Research is now emerging about how students use textbooks and how textbook use may influence student performance (Gurung, 2004, 2005; Gurung, Weidert, & Jeske, 2010). This type of research is important to those instructors who would prefer to base textbook selection on empirical data from student-learning outcomes. Three lines of research emerge: (a) how students use the textbook, (b) how textbook features affect student opinion and student course performance, and (c) the use of student opinions as part of the actual textbook selection process.

Various methodologies have been developed to empirically assess the readability of textbook passages, and textbook readability is a key selection variable by instructors. For instance, Gillen (1973) included a direct comparison of Flesch readability and human interest scores of 34 introductory psychology textbooks and found a strong correlation (+0.60) between readability and human interest scores. Such measures may be of interest to faculty members making textbook selections. Using a different student-based approach, Stang (1975) developed an assessment instrument for the evaluation of 28 social psychology textbooks, and Fernald (1989) reported that when students studied textbook material they preferred the narrative mode (storytelling) versus the traditional format when given the choice. For the final exam, mean scores were higher for the narrative approach, and information from the narrative condition was recalled more often in follow-up testing. Nevid and Carmony (2002) varied the presentation of textbook chapter material in either the traditional format and layout or a more compartmentalized modular format with individual headings used for organizational purposes. Students who indicated a preference for the modular format scored better on quiz-type questions in the modular format compared with students with no preference. These studies not only illustrate the utility of research with students but also point to the complexity of textbook selection—it is unlikely that one uniform textbook selection rubric can best suit all students' needs in all courses and situations.

Many researchers have taken the approach of asking students about various pedagogical aids and the extent to which students believe that textbook features positively or negatively impact textbook use. Weiten, Guadagno, and Beck (1996) asked students about their familiarity, their probability of use, and the overall value of 13 pedagogical aids. Students valued boldfaced terms, chapter summaries, and running glossaries the most. Weiten, Deguara, Rehmke, and Sewell (1999) replicated and extended these findings with high school, community college, and university students. Across the 15 possible pedagogical aids, boldfaced terms, running or chapter glossaries, chapter summaries, and self-tests were most valued, regardless of institutional type. In a variation of this approach, Marek, Griggs, and Christopher (1999) asked first-semester and senior-year psychology students to rate 15 pedagogical aids on familiarity, likelihood of use, and value but also conducted an analysis of 37 introductory psychology textbooks at the same time to examine the relationship between student opinion and prevalence of the feature in textbooks. Marek et al. (1999) formed two conclusions: (a) students tend to highly value pedagogical aids that are most closely associated with exam preparation, such as boldfaced type and glossaries; and (b) students tend to place lesser value on pedagogical aids designed to instill deeper learning, such as chapter outlines or discussion questions. How students interact with their textbooks and how students learn and retain information is therefore not connected (Marek et al., 1999). Weiten et al. (1996) clearly identified this disconnect when they said that "it is time to begin basic research to determine whether specific textbook pedagogical aids actually facilitate student learning" (p. 106).

Gurung directly examined the relationship between pedagogical aids and student performance (see Gurung & Daniel, 2005, for a summary). For example, Gurung (2003) asked students about the frequency of use of pedagogical aids and their perceived helpfulness, but when these student ratings were compared with exam scores, the only significant result was that there was a negative correlation (−0.20) between the ratings of helpfulness of key terms and exam performance. Thus, the overreliance on a particular pedagogical aid such as key terms may lead to detrimental influence on exam performance. Speculatively, it could be that relying on a shortcut such as studying the key terms does not lead to deeper learning. For those selecting textbooks, pedagogical aids would be assumed to enhance learning. However, these findings indicate that students may not choose to use pedagogical aids as originally intended. Gurung (2004) reported that more-able students (determined by ACT scores and high school GPA) use key terms, practice questions, and summaries less often than less-able students. In textbook selection, the specific student population should be considered when evaluating different pedagogical features. Additionally, students may require instruction on how to appropriately use pedagogical aids to facilitate deeper learning and retention. Textbook selection with particular features may necessitate an "orientation to studying" from the instructor to maximize a textbook's effectiveness.

The research previously described is invaluable in gaining an understanding of the interplay between students, textbooks, and learning. Other studies have focused more on the selection component of textbook selection than on the content itself. For example, Yonker et al. (2007) described a process for combining the opinions of instructors and students for textbook selection, and Lowry and Moser (1995) shared a multistep selection approach that was successfully used by a textbook selection committee. Regarding selection, student judgments about learning from textbooks are accurate reflections of actual learnability (Britton, Van Dusen, Gulgoz, Glynn, & Sharp, 1991) and text quality (Durwin & Sherman, 2008).

A departmental process involving students in selecting an introductory psychology textbook with successful implementation was developed by Altman et al. (2006). On the basis of faculty opinion, these researchers developed five criteria for textbook selection: content, pedagogy, student ancillaries, instructor ancillaries, and publisher's representative supportiveness. Assembling over 40 introductory psychology textbooks, faculty members each rated each textbook on the five criteria; on the basis of overall scores, the textbooks being considered for adoption were reduced to 10. Further examination of the ancillaries reduced the 10 textbooks under consideration to four. Next, one faculty member taught four sections of an introductory psychology course, with a different book being used by each section; the syllabi, lectures, class demonstrations, and exams were all identical. In fact, publishers loaned books and ancillary materials to all students so that there would be no differential costs to students, depending on their particular textbook. Average test grades and final course grades were nearly identical across the four sections; however, two sections of the course required greater assistance from the instructor because the textbooks used had graphical and pedagogical features that were more distracting than helpful. In the end, the department adopted both of the books deemed superior by students—"one book outstanding for students who were self-identified or identified by the instructor as text-oriented learners, whereas the other seemed more appropriate for learners with symbolic thinking styles" (p. 229). Given the complexity of textbook choices and the various learning preferences of students, this rigorous vetting process followed by the selection of multiple textbooks appears to be an insightful approach for textbook selection (see also McKeachie, 2002).

# RESEARCH ON NONTEXTBOOK READINGS

What if the purposeful decision is made not to use a textbook? The published literature on the use of readings is sparse in comparison with the work available on textbook selection. It is likely that there is no perfect textbook for any situation (Swales, 2009), which may lead some to consider readings. Hobson (2004) suggested that readings may be the superior choice when (a) there is a high amount of overlap between in-class lecture and the textbook, and the textbook may therefore be redundant; (b) no existing textbook is a good fit for the course; or (c) no textbook is deemed essential, but recommended readings can be placed on library reserve. Johnson and Carton (2006) pointedly suggested the following reasons for not using the full-length textbook: (a) the textbook incurs heavy reading demands; (b) reading deeply from textbooks may be a challenge; and (c) the amount of time to read full-length chapters is not conducive to student study habits, which may lead to delayed studying or cramming.

As an instructor, if the previously mentioned concerns are motivation to select a set of readings rather than use a textbook, then by what criteria should readings be selected? Much of the same criteria identified with textbooks also apply to readings. Accuracy, currency of content, difficulty level, cost, size, and format and layout are considerations that Davis (1993) recommended. A number of different approaches are available to satisfy these criteria. Open source and freely available online resources provide a wealth of resources for instructors and students (Buczynski, 2007). A classic set of readings can be used as the primary source material for an introductory psychology course (Griggs & Jackson, 2007). Smaller paperback books can be used as a central organizing theme for the introductory course, typically centering on application of research (Duntley, Shaffer, & Merrens, 2008; Gernsbacher, Pew, Hough, & Pomerantz, 2011; Hock, 2009) or debunking myths and misperceptions about psychology (Lilienfeld, Lynn, Ruscio, & Beyerstein, 2010; Stanovich, 2010). The selection of any materials for the introductory course, whether it be via textbook selection or a collection of readings, should involve a premeditated course design process in which student characteristics and learning goals are carefully weighed by the instructor.

# CONCLUSION

Depending on your experience, preferences emerge—more experienced faculty tend to want more diagrams and figures, whereas less experienced faculty rely more on the ancillary package available. Textbook selection must

## EXHIBIT 7.1
### Evidence-Based Recommendations

- Although book chapters and teaching compendia may offer sage advice, look for guidelines that are based on recommendations from empirical articles and do not solely rely on author opinion and/or expertise. Journal articles may be more empirical and timely than book chapters.
- Beware of marketing materials from publishers about the effectiveness of textbooks—look for evidence-based design of textbooks and textbook features.
- Think about the role of the textbook before you decide whether to base your textbook selection on objective physical features. Objective physical features may be easy to compare among different books, but there is little research that suggests that a book with fewer pages, more tables, or psychodynamic key terms will result in improved student learning.
- Determine whether faculty opinions or student opinions are more valuable to you as an aid in textbook selection. Students tend to prefer textbooks with pedagogical aids that assist in exam preparation; faculty members tend to prefer textbooks with the most current research.

be made with local context in mind, as well as the plan for teaching the course and how the textbook will be used in the overall course design. However, solid evidence-based recommendations here are difficult because in the literature some outcomes may be laboratory based, nearly all studies are single institution efforts, and pedagogy studies are correlational at best. Exhibit 7.1 provides recommendations for selecting a textbook or reading for a class. Exhibit 7.2 lists some key areas for future research. As educators better understand student learning and assess learning outcomes accurately, combining preexisting knowledge about effective pedagogy with an empirical scholarship of teaching and learning approach should yield educational strategies that enhance understanding of how students learn and retain information from textbooks and readings.

## EXHIBIT 7.2
### Questions for Future Research

- What decision-making rubrics do faculty follow to select the textbook?
- Does selection methodology affect the effectiveness of course materials?
- How do textbook pedagogy and student use of the textbook affect actual student performance on tests/quizzes on which the grade "counts"? The translation from laboratory to classroom may not be seamless.
- How does the course material impact student performance?
- How does student performance with readings differ from student performance with a textbook?

# REFERENCES

Altman, W. S., Ericksen, K., & Pena-Shaff, J. B. (2006). An inclusive process for departmental textbook selection. *Teaching of Psychology, 33,* 228–231. doi:10.1207/s15328023top3304_2

Bartlett, L. E., & Morgan, J. A. (1991). *Choosing the college textbook: A textbook selection checklist for instructor use.* Fort Lauderdale, FL: Nova University. (ERIC Document Reproduction Service No. ED365197)

Britton, B. K., Van Dusen, L., Gulgoz, S., Glynn, S. M., & Sharp, L. (1991). Accuracy of learnability judgments for instructional texts. *Journal of Educational Psychology, 83,* 43–47. doi:10.1037/0022-0663.83.1.43

Buczynski, J. A. (2007). Faculty begin to replace textbooks with "freely" accessible online resources. *Internet Reference Services Quarterly, 11,* 169–179. doi:10.1300/J136v11n04_11

Chatman, S. P., & Goetz, E. T. (1985). Improving textbook selection. *Teaching of Psychology, 12,* 150–152. doi:10.1207/s15328023top1203_9

Christopher, A. (2006). Selecting a text and using publisher-produced courseware: Some suggestions and warnings. In W. Buskist & S. F. Davis (Eds.), *Handbook of the teaching of psychology* (pp. 36–40). Malden, MA: Blackwell. doi:10.1002/9780470754924.ch6

Christopher, A. N., Griggs, R. A., & Hagans, C. L. (2000). Social and abnormal psychology textbooks: An objective analysis. *Teaching of Psychology, 27,* 180–189. doi:10.1207/S15328023TOP2703_04

Davis, B. (1993). *Tools for teaching.* San Francisco, CA: Jossey-Bass.

Dowie, W. (1981). Rating your rhetoric text. *College Composition and Communication, 32,* 47–56. doi:10.2307/356344

Dunn, D. S., Brewer, C. L., Cautin, R. L., Gurung, R. A. R., Keith, K. D., McGregor, L. N., . . . Voigt, M. J. (2010). The undergraduate psychology curriculum: Call for a core. In D. F. Halpern (Ed.), *Undergraduate education in psychology: A blueprint for the future of the discipline* (pp. 47–61). Washington, DC: American Psychological Association. doi:10.1037/12063-003

Duntley, J., Shaffer, L., & Merrens, M. R. (2008). *Research stories for introductory psychology* (3rd ed.). Boston, MA: Pearson/Allyn & Bacon.

Durwin, C. C., & Sherman, W. M. (2008). Does choice of college textbook make a difference in students' comprehension? *College Teaching, 56,* 28–34. doi:10.3200/CTCH.56.1.28-34

Fernald, L. D. (1989). Tales in a textbook: Learning in the traditional and narrative modes. *Teaching of Psychology, 16,* 121–124. doi:10.1207/s15328023top1603_4

Fink, L. D. (2003). *Creating significant learning experiences: An integrated approach to designing college courses.* San Francisco, CA: Wiley/Jossey-Bass.

Gernsbacher, M. A., Pew, R. W., Hough, L. M., & Pomerantz, J. R. (Eds.). (2011). *Psychology and the real world: Essays illustrating fundamental contributions to society.* New York, NY: Worth.

Gillen, B. (1973). Readability and human interest scores of thirty-four current introductory psychology texts. *American Psychologist, 28*, 1010–1011. doi:10.1037/h0035637

Goldstein, S. B., Siegel, D., & Seaman, J. (2009). Limited access: The status of disability in introductory psychology textbooks. *Teaching of Psychology, 37*, 21–27. doi:10.1080/00986280903426290

Gorenflo, D. W., & McConnell, J. V. (1991). The most frequently cited journal articles and authors in introductory psychology textbooks. *Teaching of Psychology, 18*, 8–12. doi:10.1207/s15328023top1801_2

Griggs, R. A. (2006). Selecting an introductory textbook: They are not "all the same." In D. S. Dunn & S. L. Chew (Eds.), *Best practices for teaching introduction to psychology* (pp. 11–23). Mahwah, NJ: Erlbaum.

Griggs, R. A., Bujak-Johnson, A., & Proctor, D. L. (2004). Using common core vocabulary in text selection and teaching the introductory course. *Teaching of Psychology, 31*, 265–269.

Griggs, R. A., & Jackson, S. L. (2007). Classic articles as primary source reading in introductory psychology. *Teaching of Psychology, 34*, 181–186. doi:10.1080/00986280701498582

Griggs, R. A., Jackson, S. L., Christopher, A. N., & Marek, P. (1999). Introductory psychology textbooks: An objective analysis and update. *Teaching of Psychology, 26*, 182–189. doi:10.1207/S15328023TOP260304

Griggs, R. A., Jackson, S. L., Marek, P., & Christopher, A. N. (1998). Critical thinking in introductory psychology texts and supplements. *Teaching of Psychology, 25*, 254–266. doi:10.1080/00986289809709711

Griggs, R. A., Jackson, S. L., & Napolitano, T. J. (1994). Brief introductory psychology textbooks: An objective analysis. *Teaching of Psychology, 21*, 136–140. doi:10.1207/s15328023top2103_1

Griggs, R. A., & Koenig, C. S. (2001). Brief introductory psychology textbooks: A current analysis. *Teaching of Psychology, 28*, 36–40. doi:10.1207/S15328023TOP2801_09

Griggs, R. A., & Marek, P. (2001). Similarity of introductory psychology textbooks: Reality or illusion? *Teaching of Psychology, 28*, 254–256. doi:10.1207/S15328023TOP2804_03

Griggs, R. A., Proctor, D. L., & Cook, S. M. (2004). The most frequently cited books in introductory psychology. *Teaching of Psychology, 31*, 144–147.

Gurung, R. A. R. (2003). Pedagogical aids and student performance. *Teaching of Psychology, 30*, 92–95. doi:10.1207/S15328023TOP3002_01

Gurung, R. A. R. (2004). Pedagogical aids: Learning enhancers or dangerous detours? *Teaching of Psychology, 31*, 164–166. doi:10.1207/s15328023top3103_1

Gurung, R. A. R. (2005). How do students really study (and does it matter)? *Teaching of Psychology, 32*, 238–240.

Gurung, R. A. R., & Daniel, D. (2005). Evidence-based pedagogy: Do text-based pedagogical features enhance student learning? In D. Dunn & S. L. Chew (Eds.),

*Best practices for teaching introduction to psychology* (pp. 41–55). Mahwah, NJ: Erlbaum.

Gurung, R. A. R., Weidert, J., & Jeske, A. S. (2010). A closer look at how students study (and if it matters). *Journal of the Scholarship of Teaching and Learning, 10,* 28–33.

Hartley, C. L., & Ross, A. G. (1985). Taking the guesswork out of choosing textbooks. *Nursing & Health Care, 6,* 441–444.

Hobson, E. H. (2004). *Getting students to read: Fourteen tips* (IDEA Paper No. 40). Manhattan, KS: Kansas State University, Center for Faculty Evaluation and Development.

Hock, R. R. (2009). *Forty studies that changed psychology: Explorations into the history of psychological research* (6th ed.). Upper Saddle River, NJ: Pearson/Prentice-Hall.

Johnson, E., & Carton, J. (2006). Introductory psychology without the big book. In D. S. Dunn & S. L. Chew (Eds.), *Best practices for teaching introduction to psychology* (pp. 83–92). Mahwah, NJ: Erlbaum.

Landrum, R. E. (1993). Identifying core concepts in introductory psychology. *Psychological Reports, 72,* 659–666. doi:10.2466/pr0.1993.72.2.659

Landrum, R. E., & Hormel, L. (2002). Textbook selection: Balance between the pedagogy, the publisher, and the student. *Teaching of Psychology, 29,* 245–248.

Lilienfeld, S. O., Lynn, S. J., Ruscio, J., & Beyerstein, B. L. (2010). *50 great myths of popular psychology: Shattering widespread misconceptions about human behavior.* Malden, MA: Wiley-Blackwell.

Lowry, J. R., & Moser, W. C. (1995). Textbook selection: A multistep approach. *Marketing Education Review, 5(3),* 21–28.

Lucas, S. G., & Bernstein, D. A. (2005). *Teaching psychology: A step-by-step guide.* Mahwah, NJ: Erlbaum.

Marek, P., & Griggs, R. A. (2001). Useful analyses for selecting a cognitive psychology textbook. *Teaching of Psychology, 28,* 40–44.

Marek, P., Griggs, R. A., & Christopher, A. N. (1999). Pedagogical aids in textbooks: Do college students' perceptions justify their prevalence? *Teaching of Psychology, 26,* 11–19. doi:10.1207/s15328023top2601_2

Matlin, M. W. (1997). Distilling psychology into 700 pages: Some goals for writing an introductory psychology textbook. In R. J. Sternberg (Ed.), *Teaching introductory psychology: Survival tips from the experts* (pp. 73–90). Washington, DC: American Psychological Association.

Matlin, M. W. (2002). Cognitive psychology and college-level pedagogy: Two siblings that rarely communicate. *New Directions for Teaching and Learning, 89,* 87–103. doi:10.1002/tl.49

Matthews, J. R., & Davis, S. F. (1999). An introduction to textbook publishing: What we did not learn in graduate school. *Teaching of Psychology, 26,* 40–42. doi:10.1207/s15328023top2601_8

McKeachie, W. J. (2002). *McKeachie's teaching tips: Strategies, research, and theory for college and university teachers.* Boston, MA: Houghton Mifflin.

Myers, D. G. (2007). Teaching psychological science through writing. *Teaching of Psychology, 34,* 77–84. doi:10.1080/00986280701291283

Nevid, J. S., & Carmony, T. M. (2002). Traditional versus modular format in presenting textual material in introductory psychology. *Teaching of Psychology, 29,* 237–238.

Quereshi, M. Y. (1993). The contents of introductory psychology textbooks: A follow-up. *Teaching of Psychology, 20,* 218–219. doi:10.1207/s15328023top2004_4

Robinson, D. H. (1994). Textbook selection: Watch out for "inconsiderate" texts. In K. W. Pritchard & R. M. Sawyer (Eds.), *Handbook of college teaching: Theory and applications* (pp. 415–422). Westport, CT: Greenwood Press.

Stang, D. J. (1975). Student evaluations of twenty-eight social psychology texts. *Teaching of Psychology, 2,* 11–15. doi:10.1207/s15328023top0201_3

Stanovich, K. E. (2010). *How to think straight about psychology* (9th ed.). Boston, MA: Pearson/Allyn & Bacon.

Swales, J. M. (2009). When there is no perfect text: Approaches to the EAP practitioner's dilemma. *Journal of English for Academic Purposes, 8,* 5–13. doi:10.1016/j.jeap.2008.11.003

Weiten, W. (1988). Objective features of introductory psychology textbooks as related to professors' impressions. *Teaching of Psychology, 15,* 10–16. doi:10.1207/s15328023top1501_2

Weiten, W., Deguara, D., Rehmke, E., & Sewell, L. (1999). University, community college, and high school students' evaluations of textbook pedagogical aids. *Teaching of Psychology, 26,* 19–21. doi:10.1207/s15328023top2601_3

Weiten, W., Guadagno, R. E., & Beck, C. A. (1996). Students' perceptions of textbook pedagogical aids. *Teaching of Psychology, 23,* 105–107. doi:10.1207/s15328023top2302_8

Weiten, W., & Wight, R. D. (1992). Portraits of a discipline: An examination of introductory psychology textbooks in America. In A. E. Puente, J. R. Matthews, & C. L. Brewer (Eds.), *Teaching psychology in America: A history* (pp. 453–504). Washington, DC: American Psychological Association. doi:10.1037/10120-020

Wiggins, G., & McTighe, J. (1998). *Understanding by design.* Upper Saddle River, NJ: Merrill Prentice Hall.

Winne, P. H., & Nesbit, J. C. (2010). The psychology of academic achievement. *Annual Review of Psychology, 61,* 653–678. doi:10.1146/annurev.psych.093008.100348

Yonker, J. E., Cummins-Sebree, S., Marshall, J., & Zai, R., III. (2007). Hit the books: Student and instructor surveys for psychology textbook selection, fine-tuning the process. *AURCO Journal, 13,* 81–101.

Zechmeister, J. S., & Zechmeister, E. B. (2000). Introductory textbooks and psychology's core concepts. *Teaching of Psychology, 27,* 6–11. doi:10.1207/S15328023TOP2701_1

# 8

# ARE YOU REALLY ABOVE AVERAGE? DOCUMENTING YOUR TEACHING EFFECTIVENESS

JANE S. HALONEN, DANA S. DUNN, MAUREEN A. McCARTHY,
AND SUZANNE C. BAKER

Legendary higher education scholar K. Pat Cross (1977) wryly observed that faculty regularly demonstrate vulnerability to a familiar phenomenon: the all-too-human tendency to draw faulty and inflated conclusions about the quality of their own performance. In her survey of faculty views on teaching, she found that "faculty members reveal what may as well be starkly labeled smug satisfaction. An amazing 94 percent rate themselves as above average teachers, and 68 percent rank themselves in the top quarter on teaching performance" (pp. 9–10). The tendency to believe that we are all above average may not be as outrageous as it seems. For example, in a pioneering study of over 400,000 college teachers, only 12% of the sample received below-average ratings from students (Centra, 1979).

Generating data at the end of every term, comprehensive course evaluations have become predictable practice for evaluating teaching effectiveness in most university operations. In some university settings, other feedback opportunities exist, including peer reviews, supervisor observations, and consultations with teaching specialists (Svinicki & McKeachie, 2011). Another approach to documenting teaching effectiveness depends more on the results of student experience (i.e., assessment of student learning outcomes) in the course rather than opinion of various critics (Middaugh, 2001).

The purpose of this chapter is to improve faculty capacity for making the most effective arguments regarding their teaching accomplishments. We integrate insights from self-assessment research with scholarship of teaching and learning (SoTL) literature on evidence of teaching effectiveness in an effort to offer a more nuanced approach to evaluating faculty performance. We provide some strategies to enhance the ability to self-assess accurately through SoTL research in one's classroom and how to use that evidence and one's insights to develop persuasive arguments about teaching quality to influence faculty evaluation outcomes (e.g., favorable promotion and tenure decisions, merit raise judgments). We suggest that faculty need to be proactive in constructing meaning from their professional experiences and to use self-assessment. We conclude by suggesting fertile strategies for additional SoTL research on faculty performance.

## SELF-ASSESSMENT CHALLENGES IN TEACHING

Loacker (2000) defined *self-assessment* as the process of observing, analyzing, and judging one's performance against established standards while identifying ways to improve the performance. Such assessment activities require faculty to observe and evaluate their teaching performance carefully by comparing it with available standards. These standards can come in two forms: those maintained by the faculty member's department and those held by the wider institution. In ideal situations, faculty members begin their careers in settings where the standards at each level are clear, accessible, and understandable. Yet our goal here is not to discuss the faculty review process, how such reviews are done, or even how to prepare for such evaluations (see, e.g., Dunn, McCarthy, Baker, & Halonen, 2011; Seldin & Miller, 2009); instead, we want to examine the challenges faculty face when they reflect on their own performance. Dunn et al. (2004) stressed that self-assessment emphasizes both disciplined self-regulation and self-reflection skills.

Because the literature on self-assessment is extensive and crosses many subfields within the discipline of psychology, our goal is to highlight the most relevant observations. Taylor and Brown (1994) made a persuasive case that excessively positive self-evaluation has adaptive value; research illustrating the tendencies to produce overblown assessments of one's own performance is plentiful (for a review, see Dunning, Heath, & Suls, 2004). Self-assessment can be particularly problematic when the focus of evaluation is not defined in a targeted fashion; in general, people are apt to rate themselves as "above average" on whatever dimension is being considered (Weinstein, 1980), including teaching (Cross, 1977). People reach unjustified levels of confidence about the validity of their own judgments and are routinely overoptimistic when it comes to completing tasks to meet a deadline (Buehler, Griffin, & Ross, 1994). Dunning et al. (2004) concluded that the correlation between self-assessment and skill is at best "moderate to meager" (p. 69).

In addition to having difficulties in knowing ourselves well, our ability to make objective comparisons of ourselves with others is also limited. Available research (Dunning et al., 2004) has indicated that when making statements about how one's own performance compares with that of others, it is relatively easy to overlook the successful characteristics of others in the same comparison pool. Self-assessors may also come to flawed conclusions by selectively incorporating the most flattering feedback. Worse still, perhaps, people generally assume their own self-assessments are less biased than the self-assessments made by peers (Pronin, Lin, & Ross, 2002).

According to Dunning et al. (2004), two broad psychological mechanisms account for people's biased self-assessments: lack of access to information that would lead to accurate self-assessments and a proclivity either to neglect or to give too little weight to valid information when it is available. Dunning et al. also noted that feedback from organizations tends to be unhelpful because it is given infrequently, perceived as threatening, often sugarcoated by supervisors, and delivered too late to be of any real value.

In academic settings, faculty rarely have access to data that would make accurate comparative judgments possible. Unless they spend time reading the curriculum vitae of their colleagues or happen to serve on an evaluation committee, faculty members may not be completely knowledgeable about the work and accomplishments of their colleagues. Additionally, personnel evaluations typically are confidential matters. These factors complicate any efforts that individuals may make to compare themselves with others in an objective manner.

## STRATEGIES FOR DEVELOPING BETTER SELF-ASSESSMENT SKILLS

Given these challenges, how can colleagues develop better self-assessment skills? Currently, very little research addresses how to become appropriately calibrated in the self-assessment process. Still, as self-assessors, faculty members could begin by identifying what they actually know, and do not know, about themselves; seeking such balance may temper rosy performance portrayals. Colleagues should strive to be more open to peer feedback, particularly feedback offered by supervisors (Dunn, McCarthy, Baker, Halonen, & Boyer, 2011).

In addition to constructive peer comments, reliance on performance benchmarks, too, is one way to improve self-evaluations (Dunn, McCarthy,

Baker, & Halonen, 2011; Dunn, McCarthy, Baker, Halonen, & Hill, 2007). Faculty members can evaluate the quality of teaching materials that they may have developed for their courses according to acceptable benchmarks. For example, the university may publish standards for the elements that compose an effective syllabus. To the degree that a faculty member incorporates those elements when under review, a syllabus can serve as an artifact of effective teaching that meets or exceeds the institutional benchmark.

## Teaching Portfolio

Efforts to develop better self-assessment skills can help teachers develop into more reflective practitioners, with professionals engaging in an ongoing analysis of their career experiences to learn and draw meaning from them (e.g., Johns, 2009; Schön, 1995). Recognition of this principle has contributed to the popularity of the teaching portfolio as a device to enhance teaching effectiveness (Bernstein et al., 2006; Seldin, 2004; Zubizarreta, 2009). The evidence for teaching effectiveness can include teaching evaluations, critical reviews, assessment results, and other performance indicators. Perhaps the most important element of the portfolio is the self-analysis that knits the evidence together to create an effective argument for teaching quality. Reflective teachers continually examine their efforts in the classroom as a way to identify what approaches work best for students while understanding that there is no single best way to teach (or be a faculty member in general; e.g., Seldin, 2004; Zubizarreta, 2009). Using reflection also involves the appropriate interpretation of student evaluations.

## Role of Student Feedback

The use of student evaluations as a true measure of teaching quality has been a controversial issue, generating a substantial range of opinion regarding their validity and effectiveness (Beyers, 2008; Eckert & Dabrowski, 2010; Germain & Scandura, 2005; Greenwald, 1997; McKeachie, 1997). Despite the controversy, student ratings persist as a primary measure of teaching effectiveness. Additionally, the emergence of social networks, such as Rate My Professors (http://www.ratemyprofessors.com), dedicated to review of teaching performance, underscores the prominence of the practice. Colardarci and Kornfield (2007) found a strong positive correlation between Rate My Professors ratings and formal student evaluations sponsored by the institution.

Critics of student evaluations emphasize multiple objections. An early theme in SET (student evaluation of teaching) research was the likelihood that faculty members might downgrade their standards in the hopes of increasing favorable evaluations. However, meta-analyses have confirmed that this threat is minimal. Favorable evaluations may reflect personal popularity rather than teaching effectiveness (Clayson & Sheffet, 2006).

Although student evaluations provide one perspective regarding faculty performance, student feedback does not necessarily provide pronounced evidence of learning. A recent controlled study found a small but still statistically reliable and positive relationship between students' ratings of a course and their learning gains from a course pretest through a high-stakes final exam (Marks, Fairris, & Beleche, 2010; see also Glenn, 2010). What items mattered most? The three most influential predictors were "The instructor was clear and understandable," "The supplementary materials (e.g., films, slides, guest lectures, web pages, etc.) were informative," and "The course over all as a learning experience was excellent." Interestingly, the least predictive items were "The syllabus clearly explained the structure of the course," "The exams reflected material covered during the course," and "The instructor respected the students." And course evaluations do not take into account subsequent student reflection on a course experience. Thus, for example, students may criticize a challenging professor for rigorous standards in student evaluations only to discover at a later date how much the rigor helped them to learn. Even if such post hoc evaluations were tapped in alumni letters, their impact would be viewed differently from "live" course evaluations.

According to Greenwald (1997), advocates for student evaluation believe that there is sufficient evidence of convergence from multiple sources to warrant confidence in the continued use of the students' viewpoint. Although ratings may be contaminated by factors other than teaching quality, the effects of such bias are likely to be minimal. McKeachie (1997) argued that a positive correlation between effectiveness ratings and student grades logically should transpire because the students who fared best in the course should be in a good position to attribute appropriate credit to the teaching that helped them succeed. He also argued against using student evaluations as a sole measure of teaching effectiveness and expressly discouraged the practice of averaged student ratings across courses to produce an overall teaching effectiveness rating.

Online course delivery has created additional challenges for interpreting students' views of teaching quality. Pallett (2006) summarized several advantages, including realizing efficiency in processing from direct transcription of student comments and saving class time that would have been dedicated to a paper-and-pencil review. On the negative side, online review systems tend to reduce response rates, enhancing concerns regarding the validity of student feedback. Adams and Umbach (2010), for example, found that students earning low grades (Ds, Fs) in a course were 23% less likely than other students to complete the online evaluation forms. They also found that student response rates were apt to be 6 percentage points higher for major courses than for elective or other courses.

Further, loss of administrative controls over the process may render the results vulnerable in other ways. For example, a 2-week period of online access to the evaluations for any given class may produce mixed results from the students, some of whom may be responsive to receiving disappointing exam results returned late in the evaluation time frame. Students may also display "survey fatigue" when their institutions pepper them with too many online surveys—including course evaluations—during a semester (Adams & Umbach, 2010). Despite the difficulties, many campuses are pursuing online systems.

Even the best professors have felt the distinctive, exquisite pain that comes from an unexpected harsh review from students. Faculty can take some comfort in the notion that harsh reviews are a fact of life even among the best faculty. Nevertheless, on the basis of conclusions drawn from SoTL research on faculty performance, we recommend the following strategies for addressing student evaluations of teaching so as to limit any subsequent detrimental consequences:

1. *Review the feedback carefully.* Do not concentrate solely on the negative outlying comments, but concentrate also on comments endorsing the design and operation of the course (Svinicki & McKeachie, 2010). When patterns tend to emerge across a group of students or across classes (e.g., professor doesn't seem accessible outside of class), these items may require special attention, recognition, ownership, and planning. As such, they present "desirable difficulties" (cf. Bjork, 1994) or turbulence that generates appropriate momentum from which a reasonable action plan and appropriate professional development can grow.

2. *Compare the feedback to peer performance.* If departmental averages are available, faculty members can see the comparative data that the supervisor is using to examine performance throughout the department. The normative data can help you decide whether to ignore or attempt to explain the ratings. When institutions do not provide numerical ratings, scrutiny of narrative comments of colleagues willing to collaborate who have similar teaching assignments may be helpful.

3. *Elaborate on extenuating circumstances.* Point out any extenuating circumstances that could have influenced negative student reviews. For example, losing valuable class time to a weather or security emergency can sometimes make students cranky. Perhaps a professor's personal problems intruded into the class in a way that only hindsight can clarify.

4. *Restrict the range.* One strategy that can be useful is to recognize that any group of students will contain individuals whose response styles will be reflexively negative or positive (Pedhazur

& Schmelkin, 1991). Therefore, a more valid interpretation of performance can sometimes be achieved by lopping off the comments from the lower and upper 10%. However, should a faculty member adopt this approach to control response bias, the strategy needs to be explicitly addressed and approved by the supervisor.

5. *Examine contextual factors.* The student evaluation literature highlights variables that potentially might produce an advantage or disadvantage in student ratings. For example, in general, student ratings tend to be higher in the humanities than the natural sciences. Additional influencing factors include class size, whether the class is required or is taken as an elective, and the level of the class (i.e., upper division vs. lower division), among others (see Aleamoni, 1999, for a summary).

6. *Avoid reducing rigor to achieve favor.* Although the literature disputes this conclusion (cf. Seldin, 2004), many faculty are still inclined to believe that faculty with strong student evaluations are contributors to grade inflation. Unfortunately, student evaluation narratives can reinforce this perception when the data cumulatively convey a class dominated by entertainment rather than learning (e.g., "This class was so much fun, I didn't feel like I was working at all"). We advise faculty who have earned high ratings to preempt suspicions about grade inflation by providing evidence of high standards and rigor, showing reasonable grade distributions, or offering other evidence from assessment of learning objectives within the classroom. In this regard, SoTL activities can help illuminate what the numerical ratings mean.

7. *Address disappointing comments and numbers directly.* Faculty resilience can also be revealed by the degree to which they respond—or fail to respond—to student complaints. Speculating about the cause of unexpectedly low ratings can provide a supervisor with a more comprehensive set of data. A few negative comments might be contextually based and easily corrected.

8. *Preempt negative surprises.* Many faculty, as a regular practice, conduct a formative midsemester evaluation (MSE). By devoting some class time either to a discussion or written survey of what is working well (or not so well) in the class, the professor signals to his or her students that their opinions about improving the course do matter. When the professor takes visible steps to address areas of concern, that investment is likely to be reflected in the formal summative evaluations. To date, there has been no published report of empirical research to reinforce positive effects

of the MSE; however, some institutions (e.g., Berkeley, Princeton) have recommended MSEs for the assumed formative assistance they provide.

Student feedback is useful as an indication of the level of knowledge and enthusiasm, along with information about creative pedagogies, both of which are important indicators of effective teaching (National Research Council, 2003; Pusateri, 2012). However, information from student evaluations should be carefully considered within the self-evaluation process. Faculty should attend to consistent trends that regularly emerge in the student evaluations (e.g., talking too fast, poor organization skills) within the context of their personal circumstances and teaching philosophy.

As noted in the human resource literature (Ito et al., 1998), there is a tendency for supervisors to give undue weight to negative information when making performance evaluations that produces a negativity bias. As such, we recommend that candidates take steps to develop a persuasive argument in support of teaching quality using reasonable evidence and going beyond student evaluations.

## Beyond Student Evaluations

Although time frames and protocols differ from institution to institution, most use annual evaluation of faculty performance to incorporate multiple sources of evidence to meet several outcomes: (a) to ensure faculty receive appropriate feedback, (b) to intervene in cases in which performance does not meet local standards, (c) to facilitate rewards and recognition for high-caliber performance, and (d) to provide some indication of how the department is functioning as a whole. The format of the annual review can be quite prescriptive, including a formal assessment of whether the faculty member is on track with regard to success in his or her next high-stakes review (e.g., tenure), or the review can be informal, with limited paperwork exchanged between the candidate and supervisor. Besides a narrative summary of student course evaluations, these annual reviews can include peer comments gleaned from classroom or casual observations and review of professional activity reports, as well as the a chairperson's own performance assessment of the candidate.

Marshaling evidence to support teaching effectiveness should entail being selective and strategic. Unfortunately, many faculty suffer from the belief that "more is better." By bloating the year-end packet of information with every possible artifact that attests to quality, faculty may inadvertently contribute to a negative evaluation. Of course, faculty should be aware of local customs; in some environments, reviewers prefer to receive any and all relevant information and may become irritated if they have to make additional requests from faculty for further documentation. In others, "less" is truly perceived as "more." Additional indicators of excellence to consider for review materials might include the following:

1. *Teaching nominations, awards, or other external validations of accomplishment.* Even if you do not win the designation of "best," an award nomination can signal to a reviewer that your teaching stands out. Having peers request copies of a syllabus from an innovative course can also document a distinctive achievement.

2. *Peer evaluations.* Whether arranged by the supervisor or independently crafted by the candidate, a peer evaluation can be a persuasive source of evidence on teaching quality (see Chism, 2007). A structured review from a peer visit verifies the faculty member's quest for improvement and may help formulate goals for the future. Selecting someone from outside the discipline can allow the peer reviewer to concentrate more directly on the impact of various pedagogical strategies rather than focusing on the minutiae of the discipline itself (Chism, 2007). Negotiating with individuals who work in faculty development capacities on campus may produce rich feedback that is based on potentially greater sophistication in applying protocols and rendering helpful feedback. Peer reviews can also benefit from adopting an infrastructure of a more standard protocol (e.g., Teacher Behavior Checklist; Keeley et al., 2006) and using nationally normed approaches as benchmarks (Gurung & Schwartz, 2009).

3. *Exemplars of effective pedagogy.* Many institutions have embraced the importance of moving from more passive teaching models to activities in class that promote active learning and student engagement (Barr & Tagg, 1995). Choosing one or two exemplars, selected to illustrate key points of the faculty's teaching philosophy, can demonstrate the faculty member's willingness to take appropriate risks to improve student learning. Exemplars can include a well-written and comprehensive syllabus, assignments that clearly reflect well-tailored student learning outcomes listed in the syllabus, or other claims for gains in learning that can be supported by sound assessment data. Another data source might include testimony regarding how well prepared the students have been in subsequent courses, particularly if those gains can be directly attributed to the faculty member's efforts.

4. *Use of embedded assessment to demonstrate effectiveness.* Faculty may wish to select department-specific learning outcomes for inclusion in a course and subsequently can use the results of

assessment activities to support favorable evaluations. Linking the outcomes to measures of student learning allows faculty to identify whether students are learning or to identify areas in need of improvement (McCarthy, Niederjohn, & Bosack, 2011). Further, embedded assessments can distinguish between those who were distinguished in their critical analysis from those who were merely adequate and those who just never succeeded in developing the skill.

5. *Participation in professional development activities.* In addition to listing specific development events, faculty members can elaborate a few changes in their teaching practice that their participation in teaching activities fostered. For example, attending an on-campus IT symposium to improve the use of digital delivery of homework assignments reflects an orientation of continuous improvement. This citation can be made even more powerful when narrative provides examples of how teaching objectives change as the result of participation in the development activity.

6. *Evidence of supportive interactions with students.* A routine expression of thanks for a good lecture hardly stands out as special. On the other hand, e-mails or letters from students or colleagues that clearly establish the manner in which the faculty member went above and beyond to promote an optimal outcome for the student might provide useful data. Faculty whose workload involves indirect forms of teaching (e.g., advising, mentoring, supervising research) should advocate for formal review practices that might help capture the unique contributions these teachable moments can provide.

7. *Explanation of hazard duty.* Some assignments in departments carry additional burdens that should be factored in by conscientious supervisors. For example, some courses develop baggage because their content may be perceived as extremely hard even though the material might be critical to development in the major (e.g., research methods). Another type of hazardous duty might involve the faculty member who steps in at the last minute to teach a class on an emergency basis (e.g., for a sick colleague).

If the candidate and supervisor do not agree on the conclusions drawn by the supervisor, institutions often use a specific protocol for rebuttal and potential overturning of the supervisor's judgment by someone higher in the organizational hierarchy. Before embarking on such action, a faculty member should recognize that reviewers do not tend to be cavalier in rendering performance judgments. The faculty member should request an audience with the supervisor to ensure that the grounds for the unsatisfying review are clear before proceeding. Unless there is a strong likelihood that additional consideration will produce a change in judgment, the wiser course of action might be to forego an aggressive stance in rebuttal and instead focus on areas the supervisor cites as weak to show improvements in the subsequent year.

## STRATEGIES FOR IMPROVING SELF-EVALUATION IN TENURE AND PROMOTION

Promotion and tenure decisions set the stage for a well-earned celebration. A favorable tenure decision represents a career commitment from the institution that carries considerable financial importance. For example, achievement of tenure can contribute a lifetime salary in the neighborhood of $3 million for the average psychology professor (Rosofsky, 2010). Colleges and universities tend to have a complex set of regulations that govern tenure and promotion review, particularly because unfavorable decisions may result in litigation or grievance. The evaluation processes should be a reflection of the institution's mission and values, but institutions may vary in how easy the appropriate protocols are to navigate. Candidates can use the following strategies to enhance the likelihood of success in high-stakes personnel decisions.

1. *Seek expert advice with successful mentors.* Work with the supervisor to identify a recent candidate whose dossier produced strong favorable responses from review committees. Ask the colleague to walk through the strategies adopted and borrow the dossier to duplicate the structure that was successful. Consider formalizing a mentoring relationship with individuals who have successfully navigated the process.
2. *Follow directions.* Personnel review groups describe an assortment of problems that plague poorly designed dossiers. Reviewers complain of illegible documents, absent critical documents (e.g., departmental tenure vote results), materials housed under the wrong headings, and even pages of testimony that are upside down. Reviewing the instructions, proofreading the additions, and even asking for a critical review from an experienced colleague are all actions that can avert a negative impression about the readiness of the candidate for such a big step.
3. *Build the dossier for speedy review.* Unselective dossier construction tends to produce substantial redundant information. The goal of the candidate should be to develop the most precise argument for support of a favorable decision so reviewers can

efficiently evaluate. Along those lines, avoid using plastic paper sleeves in the construction of the dossier as it may make the pages difficult to turn and can run the risk of offending reviewers whose environmental sensitivities are offended by excessive and unnecessary plastic use.

4. *Divide and conquer.* A favorable high-stakes decision can be greatly facilitated by conducting effective annual review processes. Each year's effort should provide the basic data from which the dossier can be constructed. Systematic and solid work on an annual basis should make the development of an effective dossier less stressful.

5. *Select objective outside reviewers.* Reviewers who do not share the candidate's disciplinary background have a disadvantage in identifying the degree to which the candidate has achieved a high-quality scholarly or creative history at the institution. Therefore, choosing a well-respected individual who can render objective support in applying the performance standards will make a stronger statement than an unqualified letter of support from someone with a personal agenda (e.g., graduate advisor, coauthor). The ideal candidate to provide endorsement would be a reviewer whose personal acquaintance with the candidate is limited but who is familiar with the caliber of the candidate's scholarship. However, an extra step is warranted. Reviewers with exceedingly high standards sometimes use external letters to demonstrate how terrific they are at a cost to the candidates themselves. Screen out individuals who may have a reputation for negative bias or poor collegiality by conducting some social networking geared toward the reviewer's general demeanor about equity and support for others.

6. *Offer clarifying summaries or statistics.* Candidates for tenure and promotion should provide documentation consistent with reviewers' needs. A chart that summarizes prior annual evaluation conclusions rendered by the supervisor can be helpful, so reviewers can quickly comprehend patterns of sustained quality or improvement. Where numbers of publications may be specified, candidates can summarize those as well, highlighting venues that particularly reinforce conclusions of high-quality achievement. Candidates may also wish to provide a statement of research impact by providing the reviewers with citation indices or other data that illuminate the degree to which the candidate's ideas have been influential in the literature.

7. *Prepare for diverse backgrounds in the audience.* Those charged with making personnel decisions will differ in their disciplinary expertise. Statistical information, right down to the standard deviation, will tend to carry more weight with individuals in the sciences, whereas targeted anecdotes or personal reflections may be more persuasive for humanities colleagues. Recognize that most reviewers will not share your disciplinary background, and avoid jargon, acronyms, and other expressions that will communicate only to people of your own ilk. Explain the real significance of your accomplishments, but avoid being condescending in your explanation.

8. *Exploit service opportunities.* Professional service takes many forms and also represents an important vehicle for the faculty member to become well-known beyond the department. Especially in the early stages of their career, faculty members should strive to find service activities that are relevant to their professional background. Being selective and targeted provides the right showcase to demonstrate some distinctive individual talents and contributions. To optimize the impact of service, candidates should use their assignments to develop their leadership skills. They should follow through on assignments and take the extra step of keeping the department informed about any actions that might have an impact on department functioning. "Sitting on" committees generally will be insufficient evidence that the candidate has made a serious contribution that should influence a favorable high-stakes decision.

9. *Navigate the politics.* One strategy that candidates sometimes adopt before obtaining tenure is not to take any public positions that will engender enemies out of fear that those enemies will subvert a favorable review. Although it is always wise to be aware of workplace politics, faculty (even those not yet tenured) should remain faithful to their own values and act in concert with the decisions that flow from those values.

10. *Seek advice for trouble spots.* Over the course of several years, faculty may encounter challenges that generate records that could have an adverse effect on a positive decision. For example, a faculty member could be accused of creating a hostile environment in a class by poor choice of jokes or other disrespectful behavior. Collaborate with the supervisor to determine whether such episodes are likely to surface as part of the deliberations. If they are likely to be present in the mix of materials, the candidate should be proactive in offering a solid defense. If it

is unlikely such episodes have yielded written commentary that will be part of the deliberations, the wiser course may be to ignore the episode and trust that the process will emphasize the most salient contributions. Institutions may have explicit regulations that govern the extent to which reliance on rumor or unsubstantiated data may be prohibited.

11. *Confront and explain serious flaws and errors directly.* Review committees will be examining evidence that underscores excellent performance. Against that backdrop, less than stellar episodes in performances will stand out. Any problematic elements, such as an atypical and awful set of class evaluations or a scholarly work in process for longer than would normally be expected, should be acknowledged and explained. Avoiding negative episodes can sometimes be interpreted as glossing over or hiding part of the story, generating sometimes disproportionate attention by reviewers.

12. *Rebut with grace.* Most protocols allow faculty an opportunity to rebut unfavorable decisions. If reviewers have not identified a specific weakness on which they based a negative decision, the candidate should ask for a clarification. The candidate's supervisor may be the best person to undertake this action. The most strategic rebuttals are those that address the specific areas that prompted concerns by the reviewers and not more than that. Candidates should write rebuttals from the standpoint that additional information should clarify why the original decision could be revisited and should be reversed. Candidates should be especially careful not to adopt a strident or perturbed tone in the rebuttal, particularly if collegiality concerns undergird the negative conclusion. The best emotional stance is to express surprise and confusion in the rebuttal about adverse outcomes, gently identifying some essential information that might allow reviewers at the next stage to reverse the negative status.

## SUMMARY OF BEST PRACTICES

In this chapter, we suggest that a substantive self-evaluation process provides useful evidence of faculty performance. Because it is unlikely that student evaluations will cease to be used in the larger evaluation process, we recommended that faculty embrace the evaluation process using a proactive approach. Carefully analyzing student feedback allows a faculty member to situate the information contextually. In other words, quantitative and qualitative feedback should be considered within the context of the course, unique circumstances, and the faculty member's philosophical approach to teaching.

We also recommend that faculty incorporate additional empirical measures of teaching effectiveness. Collecting evidence of student learning through SoTL, following the best practice recommendations offered in Chapter 1 of this volume, provides a great starting point for empirical evidence of one's teaching effectiveness. Constituents concerned with education at all levels increasingly ask for evidence of student learning. Faculty can demonstrate teaching effectiveness by documenting evidence that students have acquired both content knowledge and relevant skills as a direct result of efforts put forth by the faculty member. Additional indirect evidence of teaching effectiveness can also be documented through evidence of student successes or awards and recognitions bestowed by the broader academic community.

Ultimately, evidence of effective teaching must be well documented and presented to an evaluative body. Whether the evaluation process is singular (e.g., chair, dean) or the purview of a committee of reviewers, teaching effectiveness can only be demonstrated if evidence is well documented, clearly presented, and well articulated. We urge faculty to carefully construct that evidence so that all constituents are able to evaluate the merits of individual contributions to student learning as objectively as possible. Painful though it may be at times, we should not shy away from analyzing our teaching. Socrates reportedly said, "The unexamined life is not worth living." As teacher–scholars, faculty are in an excellent position to appreciate the benefits that can come from an objective examination of their own teaching and the effects that their behaviors have on student learning. Given these factors, Exhibit 8.1

EXHIBIT 8.1
Evidence-Based Recommendations

- Provide multiple sources of evidence of effective teaching, including evidence that demonstrates student learning.
- Tell your story. Rather than simply providing a laundry list of publications, committee memberships, and courses taught, take care to document your work and accomplishments (including teaching, service, and scholarship) as part of a coherent career with a trajectory that will continue to contribute to the institution's goals.
- Be honest about the good—and the less-than-stellar—aspects of your performance. Reviewers will appreciate a thoughtful reflection on your successes as well as your stumbles (along with a discussion of how you addressed these moments). A dossier that raises questions about a faculty member's ability to have insight into his or her own performance will typically be less positively regarded.
- Be aware of your audience. This includes not only following institutional guidelines and traditions concerning how materials are presented but also taking care that your materials communicate effectively to colleagues from multiple disciplinary perspectives.

summarizes best practices for documenting your professional effectiveness in ways that demonstrate your performance to reviewers.

## IMPLICATIONS FOR SoTL RESEARCH

The premise of this chapter—the positive impact of engaging in sustained self-assessment—should produce plentiful opportunities for empirical study. Although some aspects of teaching effectiveness, such as student evaluation phenomena, have been the focus of substantial scholarly efforts, much remains to be discovered. A list of some possible arenas for new directions in research related to student evaluations is provided in Exhibit 8.2. Despite the abundance of SoTL research on teaching evaluations, research on annual review and tenure processes is much less available. Much of the process is shrouded in confidentiality; however, the sheer number of hours faculty and administrators invest in assembling and judging dossiers makes this arena a valuable one in which to pursue new directions in SoTL. Although such highly personal processes may be more difficult to examine closely, the opportunities to contribute substantive research conclusions in this area warrant attention and action.

### EXHIBIT 8.2
### Questions for Future Research

- What influence does anonymity have on generating accurate and/or civil student response?
- What is the relationship between timing of the return of test results and student evaluation process?
- If students are generally poorly motivated, how can this status be assessed and weighed to enhance evaluation validity?
- Does public access to teaching evaluation data improve performance?
- What impact do personal variables such as age or "hotness" have on student ratings?
- How does digital sophistication factor into student opinion?
- Does administering a midsemester evaluation have a positive influence on formal summative evaluations at the end of the course?
- To what extent do review committees strive to produce unanimous conclusions in high-stakes decisions?
- What weight is carried by different kinds of evidence in annual evaluation judgments?
- Can individuals from outside the discipline render reliable judgments about faculty performance?
- What strategies minimize the impact of negative episodes in a dossier?
- To what degree are ethical breaches common in confidential high-stakes decisions?
- What influence does prior success (e.g., strong reviews for performance) have on sustained positive reviews?

# REFERENCES

Adams, M. J. D., & Umbach, P. D. (2010, November). *Who doesn't respond and why? An analysis of nonresponse to online student evaluations of teaching.* Paper presented at the annual meeting of the Association for the Study of Higher Education, Indianapolis, IN.

Aleamoni, L. M. (1999). Student rating myths versus research facts from 1924 to 1998. *Journal of Personnel Evaluation in Education, 13,* 153–166. doi:10.1023/A:1008168421283

Barr, R. B., & Tagg, J. (1995, November/December). A new paradigm for undergraduate education. *Change, 27*(6), 13–25.

Bernstein, D., Burnett, A. N., Goodburn, A., & Savory, P. (2006). *Making teaching and learning visible: Course portfolios and the peer review of teaching.* San Francisco, CA: Jossey-Bass.

Beyers, C. (2008). The hermeneutics of student evaluations. *College Teaching, 56,* 102–106. doi:10.3200/CTCH.56.2.102-106

Bjork, R. A. (1994). Institutional impediments to effective training. In D. Druckman & R. A. Bjork (Eds.), *Learning, remembering, believing: Enhancing human performance* (pp. 295–306). Washington, DC: National Academies Press.

Buehler, R., Griffin, D., & Ross, M. (1994). Exploring the "planning fallacy": Why people underestimate their task completion times. *Journal of Personality and Social Psychology, 67,* 366–381.

Centra, J. A. (1979). *Determining faculty effectiveness: Assessing teaching, research, and service for personnel decisions and improvement.* San Francisco, CA: Jossey-Bass.

Chism, N. V. (2007). *Peer review of teaching: A sourcebook.* Boston, MA: Anker.

Clayson, D. E., & Sheffet, M. J. (2006). Personality and the student evaluation of teaching. *Journal of Marketing Education, 28,* 149–160. doi:10.1177/0273475306288402

Colardarci, T., & Kornfield, I. (2007, May). RateMyProfessors.com versus formal in-class student evaluations of teaching. *Practical Assessment, Research & Evaluation, 12*(6). Retrieved from http://pareonline.net/pdf/v12n6.pdf

Cross, P. K. (1977). Not can, but *will* college teaching be improved? *New Directions for Higher Education, 1977*(17), 1–15. doi:10.1002/he.36919771703

Dunn, D. S., McCarthy, M. A., Baker, S. C., & Halonen, J. S. (2011). *Using quality benchmarks for assessing and developing undergraduate programs.* San Francisco, CA: Jossey-Bass.

Dunn, D. S., McCarthy, M. A., Baker, S. C., Halonen, J. S., & Boyer, S. (2011). Understanding faculty reluctance as reactance and opportunity for persuasion: A social psychology of assessment. In D. Mashek & E. Y. Hammer (Eds.), *Empirical research in teaching and learning: Contributions from social psychology* (pp. 143–159). New York, NY: Wiley.

Dunn, D. S., McCarthy, M., Baker, S., Halonen, J. S., & Hill, G. W., IV. (2007). Quality benchmarks in undergraduate psychology programs. *American Psychologist, 62,* 650–670. doi:10.1037/0003-066X.62.7.650

Dunn, D. S., McEntarffer, R., & Halonen, J. S. (2004). Empowering psychology students through self-assessment. In D. S. Dunn, C. M. Mehrotra, & J. S. Halonen (Eds.), *Measuring up: Educational assessment challenges and practices for psychology* (pp. 171–186). Washington, DC: American Psychological Association. doi:10.1037/10807-000

Dunning, D., Heath, C., & Suls, J. (2004). Flaws in self-assessment: Implications for health, education, and the workplace. *Psychological Sciences in the Public Interest, 5*, 69–106. doi:10.1111/j.1529-1006.2004.00018.x

Eckert, J. M., & Dabrowski, J. (2010). Should value-added measures be used for performance pay? *Phi Delta Kappan, 91*(8), 88–92.

Germain, M., & Scandura, T. A. (2005). Grade inflation and student individual differences as systematic bias in faculty evaluations. *Journal of Instructional Psychology, 32*, 58–67.

Glenn, D. (2010, December 19). 2 studies shed new light on the meaning of course evaluations. *The Chronicle of Higher Education.* Retrieved from http://chronicle.com/article/2-Studies-Shed-New-Light-on/125745/

Greenwald, A. (1997). Validity concerns and usefulness of student ratings on instruction. *American Psychologist, 103*, 1182–1186.

Gurung, R. A. R., & Schwartz, E. (2009). *Optimizing teaching and learning: Pedagogical research in practice.* Malden, MA: Blackwell.

Ito, T. A., Larsen, J. T., Smith, N. K., & Cacioppo, J. J. (1998). Negative information weighs more heavily on the brain: The negativity bias in evaluation categories. *Journal of Personality and Social Psychology, 75*, 887–900. doi:10.1037/0022-3514.75.4.887

Johns, C. (2009). *Becoming a reflective practitioner* (3rd ed.). Malden, MA: Wiley-Blackwell.

Keeley, J., Smith, D., & Buskist, W. (2006). The Teacher Behaviors Checklist: Factor analysis of its utility for evaluating teaching. *Teaching of Psychology, 33*, 84–91. doi:10.1207/s15328023top3302_1

Loacker, G. (2000). *Self-assessment at Alverno College.* Milwaukee, WI: Alverno College Institute.

Marks, M., Fairris, D. H., & Beleche, T. (2010). *Do course evaluations reflect student learning? Evidence from a pre-test/post-test setting.* Unpublished working paper, University of California, Riverside.

McCarthy, M. A., Niederjohn, D., & Bosack, T. (2011). Embedded assessment: A measure of student learning and teaching effectiveness. *Teaching of Psychology, 38*(2), 78–82.

McKeachie, W. J. (1997). Student ratings: The validity of use. *American Psychologist, 52*, 1218–1225. doi:10.1037/0003-066X.52.11.1218

Middaugh, M. F. (2001). *Understanding faculty productivity: Standards and benchmarks for colleges and universities.* San Francisco, CA: Jossey-Bass.

National Research Council. (2003). *Evaluating and improving undergraduate teaching in science technology, engineering, and mathematics.* Washington, DC: National Academies Press.

Pallett, W. (2006). Uses and abuses of student ratings. In P. Seldin (Ed.), *Evaluating faculty performance: A practical guide to assessing teaching, research and service* (pp. 50–65). Bolton, MA: Anker.

Pedhazur, E. J., & Schmelkin, L. P. (1991). *Measurement, design, and analysis: An integrated approach.* Hillsdale, NJ: Erlbaum.

Pronin, E., Lin, D. Y., & Ross, L. (2002). The bias blind spot: Perceptions of bias in self versus others. *Personality and Social Psychology Bulletin, 28,* 369–381. doi:10.1177/0146167202286008

Pusateri, T. P. (2012). Teaching ethically: Ongoing improvement, collaboration, and academic freedom. In R. E. Landrum & M. A. McCarthy (Eds.), *Teaching ethically: Challenges and opportunities* (pp. 9–19). Washington, DC: American Psychological Association.

Rosofsky, I. (2010, April 27). The cop beats the professor—(when it comes to a career) [Blog post]. Retrieved from http://www.psychologytoday.com/blog/adventures-in-old-age/201004/the-cop-beats-the-professor-when-it-comes-career

Schön, D. A. (1995). *The reflective practitioner: How professionals think in action.* San Francisco, CA: Jossey-Bass.

Seldin, P. (2004). *The teaching portfolio: A practical guide to improved performance and promotion/tenure decisions* (3rd ed.). Bolton, MA: Anker.

Seldin, P., & Miller, J. E. (2009). *The academic portfolio: A practical guide to documenting teaching, research, and service.* San Francisco, CA: Jossey-Bass.

Svinicki, M., & McKeachie, W. J. (2011). *McKeachie's teaching tips: Strategies, research, and theory for college and university teachers* (13th ed.). Belmont, CA: Wadsworth.

Taylor, S. E., & Brown, J. D. (1994). Positive illusions and well-being revisited: Separating fact from fiction. *Psychological Bulletin, 116,* 21–27. doi:10.1037/0033-2909.116.1.21

Weinstein, N. D. (1980). Unrealistic optimism about future life events. *Journal of Personality and Social Psychology, 39,* 806–820.

Zubizarreta, J. (2009). *The learning portfolio: Reflective practice for improving student learning.* San Francisco, CA: Jossey-Bass.

# INDEX

# ABOUT THE EDITORS

**Beth M. Schwartz, PhD,** is Catherine Ehrman Thoresen '23 and William E. Thoresen Professor of Psychology and Assistant Dean of Randolph College. She received her PhD in cognitive psychology from the State University of New York at Buffalo in 1991. Her early work focused on factors that influence the accuracy of child witnesses, in particular how changes in the legal system can create a more age-appropriate interview for young children. In addition to her continuing interests in psychology and law, she is also involved in a research program on the scholarship of teaching and learning (SoTL). She has given over 100 professional presentations at conferences and published over 20 books, book chapters, and professional articles in peer-reviewed journals. Her work has appeared in journals such as *Law and Human Behavior* and the *Journal of the Scholarship of Teaching and Learning*. She has worked with more than 1,000 students at Randolph College. She was the founder of the Faculty Development Center, serving as faculty development coordinator from 2000 to 2007 on her campus, providing faculty with programming focused on refining one's teaching to become most effective in the classroom. With these programs, she has created an environment in which discussing SoTL is a norm. In her role as assistant dean of the college, she continues her involvement in SoTL on her own campus.

Dr. Schwartz is coauthor of *Optimizing Teaching and Learning: Practicing Pedagogical Research* (2009, with Regan A. R. Gurung) and coeditor of *Child Abuse: A Global View* (2001, with Michelle McCauley and Michelle Epstein). She is a member of the American Psychological Association (APA) and the Association for Psychological Science, a Fellow of the Society for the Teaching of Psychology (APA Division 2), and a member of the American Psychology–Law Society (AP-LS, Division 41 of APA). In addition, she served as the associate director for programming of regional conferences in the Society for the Teaching of Psychology. At Randolph College, she teaches Introduction to Psychology, Cognitive Psychology, Research Methods, and a Senior Research Capstone Course and is an award-winning teacher (2001 Randolph College Gillie A. Larew Award for Distinguished Teaching; 2006 Outstanding Teaching and Mentoring Award from AP-LS). She currently serves as chair of the Psychology Department.

**Regan A. R. Gurung, PhD,** is Ben J. and Joyce Rosenberg Professor of Human Development and Psychology at the University of Wisconsin–Green Bay (UWGB). He received his PhD in social/personality psychology from the University of Washington–Seattle in 1996. His early work focused on social support and close relationships, and he studied how perceptions of support from close others influence relationship satisfaction. His later work investigated cultural differences in coping with stressors such as HIV infection, pregnancy, and smoking cessation. Building on and continuing with his previous interests, he currently has three main areas of interest: culture and health, impression formation and clothing, and pedagogical psychology. His research on pedagogy is designed to answer the simple question: How can we optimize student learning? His research involves gaining a thorough knowledge of extant attempts to understand how students learn and focuses on three major components: student behaviors (e.g., study techniques), instructor behaviors (how is learning facilitated?), and the means by which content is transferred (textbooks and technology). Studies in progress address each of these areas. He has given more than 150 professional presentations at conferences and published nine books, 22 book chapters, and over 40 professional articles in peer-reviewed journals. His work has appeared in journals such as *Psychological Review*, *Teaching of Psychology*, and *Personality and Social Psychology Bulletin*. He has supervised over 200 undergraduate independent studies and taught more than 6,000 students at UWGB; the University of California, Los Angeles; and California State University, Long Beach. During summer 2008, he participated in the National Conference on Undergraduate Education in Psychology at the University of Puget Sound, serving as contributor to a working group concerned with optimizing the curriculum for undergraduate education in psychology.

Dr. Gurung is author of *Health Psychology: A Cultural Approach* (2nd ed., 2010) and *Optimizing Teaching and Learning: Practicing Pedagogical Research* (2009, with Beth M. Schwartz) and editor of *Culture and Mental Health: Sociocultural Influence, Theory, and Practice* (2009, with Sussie Eshun); *Getting Culture: Incorporating Diversity Across the Curriculum* (2009, with Loreto R. Prieto); and *Exploring Signature Pedagogies: Approaches to Teaching Disciplinary Habits of Mind* (2009, with Nancy L. Chick and Aeron Haynie). He is a member of the American Psychological Association (APA), a Fellow of the Society for the Teaching of Psychology (APA Division 2), chair of the Education and Training Council (part of APA Division 38), and codirector of the UWGB Teaching Scholars Program. Dr. Gurung is an award-winning teacher (UWGB Founders Award for Excellence in Teaching, Featured Faculty Award, Creative Teaching Award) and researcher (UWGB Founders Award for Excellence in Scholarship). At UWGB, he teaches Introduction to Psychology; Health Psychology; and Culture, Development, and Health. He served as national president of the Society for the Teaching of Psychology (APA Division 2) in 2011, chair of the UWGB Psychology Department from 2003–2005, associate dean of Liberal Arts and Sciences at UWGB from 2006–2008, and chair of Human Development at UWGB from 2008–2010.